Kimmy's Furry Diary

...and this time it's purrsonal

By Kimmy

An Authors OnLine Book

Text Copyright © Kimmy 2014

Cover design by Christine Wilson and James Fitt ©

All rights reserved. No part of this publication may be reproduced, stored in a retrieval system, or transmitted in any form or by any means, electronic, mechanical, photocopy, recording or otherwise, without prior written permission of the copyright owner. Nor can it be circulated in any form of binding or cover other than that in which it is published and without similar condition including this condition being imposed on a subsequent purchaser.

British Library Cataloguing Publication Data.
A catalogue record for this book is available from the British Library

ISBN 978-0-7552-0747-3

Authors OnLine Ltd
19 The Cinques
Gamlingay, Sandy
Bedfordshire SG19 3NU
England

This book is also available in e-book format, details of which are available at www.authorsonline.co.uk

With thanks to the vets and nurses at
Abbey and Clare Vets
Pete Wedderburn
and Nathalie Andrews at Girl and Cat Publishing

Foreword

by Christine Wilson

Life was pretty good for Kimmy and me after the publication of "Kimmy's Irish Diary," her second book. It had been just over a year since we came over to Northern Ireland to look after my mother. We were in our new apartment with its lovely, safe back-garden with the thick lawn, mature trees and hedges. It was very different to our Pink House in Bath, which had been a Georgian town-house, narrow and tall with lots of stairs and on a busy main road with a quiet, walled courtyard at the back. This apartment was a new-build on the ground floor of a big house that had five other flats and one big front door. It had two bedrooms, two bathrooms and a large, comfortable kitchen and living area, with a warm, soft carpet throughout and – best of all – a nice, fenced-in garden outside. It was part of a larger new development, only half finished – so we had a building site directly in front of us. Kimmy used the windows as her exit and entrance to the building rather than the front door, as she still didn't like to be seen by anyone else but me. I was able to look out of the window and watch Kimmy walking across the grass with a swagger that suggested confidence I don't think she had before. She still hid when strangers came to the door, but more and more often, she would appear when a friend came round and she would push her little head into a hand to be patted – something she'd never done before. The unpleasant people from upstairs who dared to complain about me 'keeping a cat' (despite it being allowed in my lease) moved out and their flat was empty for a while, but a newly-married couple moved in in August 2010 and they were animal lovers so there were no problems at all; we had peace and quiet to enjoy a reasonably good Irish summer with some warm days. I let Kimmy go out as much as she liked but I preferred the quieter times at the start of and end of the day when the builders working around our block had gone home. Most of the neighbours had seen Kimmy and they seemed to like her, although she always avoided them. There was a small boy, Michael, who lived down the road and he toddled along to see her, and he called her 'Kibby'. Everyone in the local village where we lived knew Kimmy because they'd read her books and the mention of her name always got a smile... Her popularity on United Cats (www. Unitedcats.com) and Facebook (The Kimmy Diaries for Fans of Kimmy) is very touching and it is amazing to think that a cat like Kimmy has fans in Israel (Debby), America (Anne, Roni and Etta), Australia (Becka), South Africa (the lovely Mara Strydom) and all over England – (Cathrine, Vonnie, Marketa and Graham, the taxi driver who brought us to Ireland from Bath), Denmark (Charlotte who has since died); there are also Etta and Connie in Canada, Christina Almeida in the Canary Isles, Anne Petzer in Prague and, of course, Jan Clare in Bath. And many many more.

We were both relaxed and happy and enjoyed living here and I even mulled over the possibility of buying one of the new houses being built opposite us, not ten yards away. Kimmy liked to stroll around them in the evenings (because they had no doors or windows yet, and they didn't have roofs either). I loved to think that she was putting a bit of herself into the building of those houses. I wasn't sure if we could face another move – even if it was just across the road – but they had private gardens and an extra tiny bedroom and I thought Kimmy would be happy with more privacy. It was maybe something we'd do in the future?

As before (with "The Kimmy Diaries" and "Kimmy's Irish Diary"), all author royalties, approximately one pound fifty per book, go to Bath Cats and Dogs Home so other animals will benefit.

Summer

22nd July 2010

'Kimmy, we're going to the vet to get you weighed. You're going to Fat Club,' yells Mum, filling me with dread. I am a beautiful tabby and white girl with a pretty, round tummy and a little tabby spot by my nose. I am thirteen and a half years old, but I don't look it because I am so well fed and my coat is so good. My fur is soft and luxurious and anyone can see that I am a much loved cat indeed. I used to live in Bath, but Christine (whom I call Mum, because she takes care of me) adopted me and later she brought me with her to Northern Ireland – all the way in a taxi because she couldn't drive and *her* Mum was hurt in a fall. And we live here now. Oh, and did I mention that I am sometimes called Countess Kimmy?

Fat Club is the cruel invention of the local V-E-T, where all the slightly-rounded cats of the area are made to get on scales and then each is given a ticking off. It is really to make our Mums fuss over us a bit more and afterwards we have to eat less food – it's very unfair.

I try to run away as soon as I hear the words, but Mum grabs me and puts my wriggling body in the carrier before I can mew a very rude word to her. She carries me out and sets me, in the carrier, on the wall dividing our neighbour from our block, so I can see around me. Carol Ann, the lady who lives next door, comes out and calls out to Mum. 'Everything OK?' she says, referring to me.

'Oh yes, fine thanks. Just taking Kimmy to the vet.'

'Is she all right?' asks the neighbour, her voice full of concern.

'Oh yes,' laughs Mum. 'She's fine. She's just going to be weighed and maybe have her teeth cleaned.'

Oh yes, tell everyone!

Gran arrives. Mum still can't drive yet and isn't able to fit me on her push-bike and, within minutes of the dread words, 'the vet,' being uttered, we are off, driving down the hill and then round the corner and up the road (oh yes, I know the way…)! Mum wants to see Naomi who only works certain days. We don't call Naomi 'Auntie Naomi' yet but we probably will soon. Mum thinks Naomi is the best vet of all, but surely it doesn't take much skill just to weigh a little thing like me?

My travel carrier is dumped first on the counter, where my name is taken. 'Kimmy for a weigh in and er…' Mum hesitates. 'Oh while we're here, let's get Naomi to look at her teeth, as they may need cleaning.'

Then my box is placed on the floor inches away from another cat in a similar situation and a dog that looks a bit over-friendly to me. Why oh why they make us all sit together when we don't really get on beats me, but I will make Mum pay for this later by ignoring her for as long as I can.

The vet's door opens and our friend Mercia comes out with her new ginger dog, Teddy. Her other dog was called Pip, but he died just recently and she cried and cried. Mum was upset too and hugged me extra close, which I quite liked. Teddy has made Mercia far happier now. He is in for a checkup. Mum brandishes a copy of *Your Cat* magazine and shows Mercia, and everyone else in the room, that my book, "Kimmy's Irish Diary" has been reviewed.

'It's not very big,' says Mercia, clearly unimpressed.

Mum bristles and says something about size not mattering. She has been so pleased with it. I agree with Mum – it means a lot to be as famous as me and get mentioned in a cat magazine.

'Kimmy please!' booms the vet's voice and I try to hide in my box as I am carried in, so maybe they won't find me at all. If you've ever tried to hide in a box you will know it is not that easy, but I did a pretty good job and when Mum and the vet try to gently tip me out, I hang on tightly. But gravity prevails and I tumble out onto the counter where I reward their efforts with my most pathetic mew. I lick my lips and gaze around for an escape route, but there is none.

Mum is saying something about my book, "Kimmy's Irish Diary," which has just come out. Naomi has just finished reading "The Kimmy Diaries" and looks pleased to get another book so fast. She is a very smiley person who always seems to remember all the cats and dogs she sees even though there must be a lot. I think she likes me best. I hope that maybe this is all we have come in for. She'll take the book and we'll go. Maybe I could autopaw it?

But no. Next, my mouth is wrenched open and Naomi is peering inside in a way that seems a little rude, although she is actually very nice to me and doesn't seem to think me as spoilt as the last vet did. 'Hmmm…' she is saying, as vets do. 'They do look a bit dirty. I see some tartar and maybe a little gingivitis…'

I have no idea what that is, but Mum seems upset. 'Oh dear, will she need to get them cleaned? I'd hate her to have an anaesthetic...'

I remember my emergency surgery a few years ago when Uncle Roger in Bath cleaned my teeth. It was dreadful and I felt rotten afterwards. They surely weren't going to do it again?

'Hmmm,' Naomi says again, feeling round my jaw. 'Have you noticed anything else?'

Mum looks embarrassed. 'She dribbles a bit.'

'Ok. Well, let's try antibiotics and see if that clears it,' says Naomi, still prodding at my jaw, much to my indignation. Then she goes off and taps on her computer. Her friendly face looks a bit crinkled as if she is thinking of something.

'Can we weigh her please?' says Mum, waving our Fat Club reminder letter. I hope Naomi will say 'No need,' but instead she carries me to the big scales in the middle of the waiting room, in front of *everyone* and those dogs... I yowl in protest as I am placed on the scale and Naomi's brow furrows. 'Oh, she's five point five kilos,' she announces to everyone in the room, but this time no one giggles and there is a gasp of joy from Mum. 'Oh, that's so good! She's lost nearly half a kilo!'

'She's still quite a substantial cat,' says Naomi, entering this momentous achievement on my records.

'Is she now a size fourteen?' enquires Mum hopefully. (She likes to think of my size in terms of what my human dress size would be.)

'A sixteen maybe...' says Naomi. 'We need to try and get her closer to five kilos.'

Yeah, yeah. Vets never accept the good things. They always look at the negative. I mean, there was I, running around the garden every day and existing on tiny rations just to lose this weight, and there was she, suggesting I should lose *more!*

Joyfully Mum pays for the horrible antibiotics, that I know I will just spit out, and I am gathered up and carried out. Soon I am back in the car and on my way home.

(Note from Christine – I was totally joyous at Kimmy's weight loss and the only thing that upset me about the mention of Kimmy's teeth was that I might have to bring her back to have them cleaned, and I couldn't bear that, as it would mean an anaesthetic and her being taken to the bigger vet's surgery, where they do the operations. There, I would have to leave her and return later, which I always hated. I should have read the signs – the dribbling and Naomi not looking as thrilled as me. I didn't and it would come back to haunt me in just a few weeks' time.

I was so relieved to be taking Kimmy home that I hadn't given a second thought to the possibility that something quite significant had happened that day.)

23rd July 2010

The good thing about taking any sort of medicine, if you're a cat, is that at least you get decent food. Mum is always so keen to disguise the taste that she gives me something delicious and, as I can't really take tablets in my dried food, she gives me nice, meaty wet stuff. So I eat the tablet without fuss and nom nom until it's all gone. Mum always praises me and gives me a cuddle and I like that.

She puts an announcement on Facebook, which we use now

instead of United Cats, telling everyone on my very own fan page (The Kimmy Diaries for Fans of Kimmy) that I've lost weight. Graham Blacker, the nice man who drove us over here from Bath, sends us a message.

Hello Kimmy, I hear you have lost weight, I wish I could do the same you clever thing. Guess what, I have read half of your latest publication "Kimmy's Irish Diaries" it was really fascinating reading about our little escapade across the Irish Sea. What a great life it must be for you over there, I hope you are really enjoying yourself and looking after Christine. Prrrrrrr

Mum is very pleased with his email and then decides she will start offering some weight loss tips to other chubbier cats. She starts by telling Graham he should buy Prescription Diet MD from the vet and run around the garden a lot. This makes her snort with laughter. I reward her by rolling on my back and showing her my tabby and cream tummy.

28th July 2010

I have a large garden to walk around: my own private back garden with a big, old tree and a colourful gnome sitting underneath it. I go there to sharpen my claws. I love the feel of the thick grass under my paws, as I never had that in Bath in our sunny courtyard at the back of the big, pink house. Sometimes the grass feels wet under my paws and they squelch over it, and sometimes it feels dry and warm or cold and frosty. But it always feels good. I have a big hedge at the back of the garden, with a gap in it where I can go to get into the grounds of the school behind. Sometimes I just go in there to 'get away' from Mum, as she can be quite demanding. Cats do need special places where we can go. Sometimes I do my 'business' there, as I don't like people to see me and this is fairly private. I don't use my litter tray so much anymore and that feels good too. If I am feeling extra adventurous, I walk across the car park to sit with the big birds that Mum calls magpies. Some of them are bigger than me and I like to just sit watching them. Or I go under a wire fence into the building site next to our flat. I walk around the corner to the new houses being built and sit out on the flower bed there (or go into the houses themselves, which are funny because they have no roof, carpets or furniture or anything, and I wonder who would want to live there) – but I just sit and I sometimes see Mum looking out of the window, watching me watching her. We cats like to watch. We can learn a lot just by sitting, staring and taking everything in.

It is a warm evening and I can feel the sun on my fur. I am thinking of the good supper waiting for me when I go in, although I had one just before I went out.

Suddenly a big black horror appears. He is disguised as a bush, but I realise I am staring at the fearsome Guinness who is sharing the same flower bed as me! You may remember that Guinness is a horrible feral cat who gets all the lady cats in the 'family way' whether they want to be or not. Every black and white cat in the area looks just like him. He can't get me 'with kitten,' as I've been 'done,' but that doesn't stop him trying! He is a massive great thing with a big, square, black face with a slash of white, and short back legs, and he must weigh about seven or eight kilos at least. He takes a

The fearful Guinness

flying leap at me with his claws extended and his big, black, ugly fur all standing on end. He has ambushed me by hiding in a plant! He's going to bash me – or, with his lady-killing reputation, perhaps he'll do worse. Oh, and because he sleeps in a ditch, he smells bad too.

I don't think about the road in front of the houses and I just run blindly. I can hear Mum yelling, 'Here Kimmy!' as she opens the window, but I am already running past her and round to the back of the house with Guinness in hot pursuit. He can run pretty fast for such a big cat, but I am faster and I just get in through the bedroom window before Mum slams it shut. And he jumps up and sits on the window ledge, hissing and spitting with fury through the glass as we watch from the safety of indoors. I start to wash myself just to show him I don't care and I feel very proud of Mum for getting me in so fast and keeping him out. But I get told off for running over the road without looking, so it seems I can never win...

I get a plate of tuna later as a peace offering and I spend the rest of the evening purring on my favourite rug.

(Note from Christine – Guinness was getting to be such a nuisance, as he was always coming round here, having followed us from our last address, and he seemed obsessed with Kimmy and trying to hurt her. I was glad I was there to rescue her and get her in safely. But secretly I also quite enjoyed these little dramas, as they added colour to the day.)

29th July 2010

While I am telling you all about road safety I have to tell you how I approach it. Usually, when I am not being chased by Guinness, I sit on the pavement and look one way and then another. Then I look the other way and back. I do this a few times to make *absolutely* sure it's safe. I crane my little neck out too, to look down the hill, and when I am happy there are no cars coming, I stroll across the road. I usually get about half way. Then I decide it is warm and sunny right there and that a little patch of sunshine has warmed the tarmac, so I lie down and roll over a few times. It feels so good to do this but then the window opens and Mum yells across the street, 'Kimmy get off that road right now!' I have to run off – in the wrong again.

30th July 2010

Mum comes home from seeing her friends, Karyn and Fred, all excited (also smelling of that funny fruity stuff that makes her all wobbly). 'Kimmy, guess what!'

I yawn.

'I met someone in the pub who came over specially to say how much she enjoyed reading your Irish Diaries!' She seems pretty pleased with this and I suppose I am too, but it's late and I want us both to go to bed so we can snuggle. That is what I like best.

31st July 2010

Mum's gone mad. She is pulling open cupboards and taking stuff out and then throwing it all into bags. I do hope we are not moving again, but Mum sees my look and assures me that we are *definitely not moving*. Then she goes off with the bags and later she opens her emails to find one from her friend Elaine – she's the one who came to visit us in Bath when I first came to live with Mum. She has a cat called Grace who looks a bit like me but is older. She says she really enjoyed my book, and Mum is thrilled. I am a bit too, I suppose, but I'd rather have some extra dinner. It turns out Mum is just having something called a 'clear out.' She's still going all tidying-crazy and I need to get out of her way before she tidies me away too.

Grace (photo by Martin Childs)

1st August 2010
Mum gets all upset because, when she is watching the box, now attached to the wall, she discovers that a 'lady off the telly' (someone she doesn't like) is younger than her. 'Do I look that old Kimmy?' she asks, worried. Well how do I know? I'm a cat!

2nd August 2010
I have already told you about the magpies that sit outside in the

car park and the garden? Well I really like to sit outside with them and just watch them. I would really like to catch one and eat it up, but even I know my limitations. I have never really caught a bird in my life, although I wish I had. I dream about it often when I am in a deep, deep sleep. I run and chase them and they never get away, but I don't suppose dreams count?

There are lots of these big black and white things and they are very big – far bigger than me. I sit outside with them for a while until I realise that they are all around me in a circle. I lick my lips, suddenly less sure of myself. This is not how it should be. I see Mum poking her head out of the window with that camera thing she is always using to take pictures of me to send her friends.

Just then, the birds get cross and all whoosh at me, and I am scared. I mean, I am not really that big anymore, what with losing nearly half a kilo, so I just run as fast as I can with the big birds running after me. You may laugh, but it is very scary indeed. I jump in the window and Mum slams it closed behind me – like she did with Guinness the other day. Safe!

Can you believe how exciting my life is?

4th August 2010

Mum has offended all the neighbours by writing them each a note or dropping by to ask them 'Not to run over my cat by mistake when you drive in and out.' I am not sure how much they like being told what to do, but none of them hit her and most are very nice about it. I think they think that my Mum is a bit batty. But I know she means well.

7th August 2010

Mum is all pleased because, when she calls for a taxi they ask her if she is 'Kimmy's Mum?' They've all read my book and love it and know Mum because of me.

I spend a busy morning looking out of the window at the garden. I don't always want to go out; sometimes I just like to look and see who's there. Mum is worried that maybe Guinness has scared me and I don't like to admit it, but he has a bit.

(Note from Christine – it was so nice to phone Abbey Taxis and be asked if I was Kimmy's Mum! Kimmy was so well-known here, but I was also slightly worried that Kimmy seemed scared to go out. What with being bullied by Guinness and now the magpies – would she ever want to go out again?)

14th August 2010

It's a beautiful hot day and Mum goes off to do something called a street collection for the Mid Antrim Animal Sanctuary, which is a bit like the Bath Cats and Dogs Home where I am from. It's another place for cats and dogs that don't have homes. She is in a good mood, as we all love the sunshine. When she comes home she tells me about the lovely drive along the coast road, but I don't really care, as she has bought me some Felix Roasted Food and I love that. She has tried me with the Prescription MD dried food again, but I really don't like it. It seems to hurt my mouth a bit and I look up at her, all disappointed, and mew for something else. After a while she gets the message.

(Note from Christine – I hadn't given Kimmy her dried food for

a while. First of all, we'd run out and then, when we got some more, I realised I couldn't conceal the antibiotics in it easily, so I bought some wet food but tried to give her smaller portions more often – so she had three small meals a day. This seemed to work for us. When I tried to get her back on the dried diet food, she refused it and I just thought 'Well she's had some more delicious food now and doesn't want her diet food. Can I blame her?' I decided to just keep her on regular pouches, either until her teeth had been cleaned or until perhaps she was showing some weight gain and we had to think again. I felt sure that it was the extra exercise doing more for her weight loss than anything else. If I had properly realised that it was giving her pain to eat dried food, I think I would have been quicker to take her back to see Naomi at the vet's again. We don't always think of these things at the right time.)

19th August 2010

Another gorgeous, hot day and everyone is in a good mood. Mum says that she should really take me back to the vet to see if the antibiotics have worked, but she has an appointment with Caroline, the solicitor-person, who is really *my* solicitor, as she represented me when those horrible people in the apartment above complained about me, and Mum had to get Caroline to write them a letter. Mum is making her will again, as she wants to make sure I am well provided for. Of course I have no idea what that means, but I like to think that she is thinking of me all the time. I also don't want to go to the vet, so if Mum is thinking of me in some other way, then that is *fine* by me. She goes off and I try to imagine life without Mum. I can't – or rather I wonder if it would be the same as her going off and not coming back. Who'd give me my dinner? Mum says that Gran would, as she has asked her, but Gran doesn't sound too keen. Oh well, as long as someone looks after me and it means I don't have to go to the vet then that is OK. I settle down for a snooze.

(Note from Christine – I had already made a will, making provision for Kimmy, but I had watched a television programme about the type of will service I had used – a will-making service where they come to your home – and the programme warned that you can't be sure it is all correct and legal. That made me think my will might not be valid and I wanted to re-make it to be sure. It was one of the most terrible ironies that, on the day I should have been taking Kimmy to Naomi's surgery on a Thursday morning, I was going to make provision for her in the event of my dying first.

But I did phone the vet that day and make an appointment for the following Thursday when I knew Naomi would be in – so I suppose that was something.)

20th August 2010

Today is Mum's birthday and she says she wants a really special day. I rub around her and ask her for breakfast and she takes the hint and obliges. Later I watch her going off on her bike and coming home with the handle bars all weighed down with bags and she is all excited. 'I've got things to give my friends tonight. They're coming to my little dinner party,' she says and I am puzzled. Aren't they supposed to give her things if it is her birthday? Well, what do I know? I am a cat and I don't even have a birthday. But she pins on a huge badge that says 'It's my birthday,' and wears a nice dress. Then she gets her hair done and comes back looking quite pretty. I have the sort of Mum who looks good when she tries a bit – sometimes a lot. Unlike me, as I am a natural beauty who doesn't have to try at all. For the rest of the day, people drop by with cards and presents and, at one point, we are both having a nap (I love napping with Mum, as I love to get really close to her and purr). She throws back the covers and goes to greet them with my fur still all over her. I hide under the bed as I always do when someone comes in – even if it is Karyn Stapleton, the nice lady with all the cats that we know from when we lived in our last flat and she was our neighbour. She and her close friend, Fred, look after me when Mum is away and they are very nice to me, although I always give them my most pathetic look as I really hate it when I am left alone. Gran has already given Mum a cushion with a cat on it and all her birthday cards have cats on or ladies getting all wobbly from that fruity stuff that smells funny. I think these are because of Mum's two favourite things – cats and wobbly-making, fruity stuff.

While she goes out to eat dinner somewhere that has a funny name – 'The Dirty Duck' – (why would anyone want to eat anywhere that was *dirty?)* I settle down for a good nap and am delighted when she comes back with some treats for me. Chicken – my favourite. Mum says she has had the best birthday ever and we both snuggle up for a good sleep. But first I do a quick circuit of the garden – before patting the window with my paw to be let in.

It's pretty well been the perfect day for us both.

21st August 2010

'Breakfast!'

I like to wake Mum around six thirty a.m. She mutters something about 'Go away Kimmy,' but I persist. I am hungry and I want to get out in the sunshine before Guinness shows up. I am also bursting for a pee and I want to do it in the garden *after* I have had my brekkie. I always like to pee *after* breakfast, as I don't like to do anything until I've eaten. She looks up and says something about me dribbling over her. 'You must be hungry,' she says. She staggers around for a while, opening packets and scraping them onto a dish for me and then goes back to bed. I come back after a walk in the garden and join her. We both get up a few hours later and this time I want a second breakfast.

22nd August 2010

It is a wonderfully hot day and Mum puts a chair and a mat outside so she can lie there. I want to take a nap, but when I look out the window and see how comfortable Mum is with the big Sunday newspaper in front of her, I feel I should join her so I take a big jump out of the window and down onto the ledge, then down to the ground. I stroll over to Mum and decide to lie on the ground too, on my back. My tummy is exposed and I throw back my head with my legs flailing in the air. Mum laughs. She loves to see me in the garden like this and I love to see her. We're not usually both in the garden at the same time – I think the last time was in Bath. But it's too hot for me really and after a while I go into the shade. Mum stays where she is and I hate to tell her that she is looking a bit red.

(Note from Christine – watching Kimmy sprawled out like that in the sun is one of my happiest memories of her. She loved sunshine and she loved me being in the garden with her – most cats like to spend time outdoors with their carers. Cats love to sunbathe and I am absolutely certain that both Kimmy and I were totally and perfectly happy on that gloriously warm day with the bright blue sky.)

23rd August 2010

Sometimes I find Mum really annoying, as she can be quite contrary when I least expect it. I am on the bed, having a really good dream, when suddenly she swoops down on me and picks me up and a moment later I am dropped into my travel carrier. I wonder how she would feel if someone picked her up while she was asleep and put her in a small box. Then I am carried out to a car – the driver of which I don't even know – and we are driving in the direction of – not the vet – but Gran's. We first stayed at Gran's when we moved over from Bath, so I am used to it. My box is opened and I stagger out, giving a hiss of objection, and I make for the back door to the garden (which I always do). I love Gran's back garden. It is very big and has a big, safe wall around it, so I feel very secure. It also has a lot of interesting smells – plants, trees, flowers and bushes and my favourite strawberry bush. I stroll around for a while and am aware that my every move is being watched and photographed as if I am a famous cat – which of course I am. I amble into 'The secret garden,' an extra bit of walled garden at the back, and this feels like my very own private place. I take a good sniff – I can smell Jamie, Gran's black and white cat.

Kimmy and 'Uncle' Jamie in the garden

Because he belongs to Gran, he is sort of a relative: my uncle – 'Uncle Jamie', and I know that he is around somewhere. I don't have to wait long to see him. He appears, as if by magic, walking very low – almost crawling along on his stomach. He is following me. I decide to ignore him until he gets a bit closer – so I send him a warning snarl – then I go inside to see if he has any interesting food for me to eat. Unfortunately Jamie's dishes all seem to be full of dried food and I am not that keen on dried food, as it hurts my jaw when I eat it. So I ignore it and yowl in protest. Mum takes the hint and appears with a saucer of acceptable food which she places in front of me. I start to eat, but I can see Jamie out of the corner of my eye, watching me. Then I see him climbing into my carrier and that is just too much. I temporarily abandon my food to go and smack Jamie hard and he cries out and runs off. I watch him go and then I go back to his, or rather *my* dinner.

Mum and Gran are now watching television and I stroll in to see if there is anything of interest for me there, but apart from saying 'Hello Kimmy,' they ignore me, so I go out again to the garden and, after another stroll, I settle down for a nap in a place where I can see out of the glass doors – a spot under a table; I can see, but I am nice and safe.

Then blow me, if she isn't in again with that carrier saying 'Come on, Kimmy – time to go home.'

Have you any idea how annoying it is to be in one place, and then you have to be moved again?

I'm not having this, so when Mum's hand comes towards me, I hiss and growl and lash out with my paw – really hard. I don't usually hit Mum, but today she really has got on my nerves! Mum yelps and pulls back her hand, which is bleeding, and calls out to Gran, 'Oh no… She doesn't want to come home!'

Gran comes in and says something about 'leave her then and come back tomorrow. Or you could stay the night?'

Mum mutters something about having 'things to do' and not having brought her overnight stuff and tries again to grab me. I repeat the paw slashing action and make the yowl louder and louder so that she gets quite alarmed. 'I think she is having a tantrum!' she says to Gran and I hiss again to confirm this. This goes on for a while until I decide to make a dash for it. I don't really want to be prodded at under the table and it looks as if she might move it to get at me more easily. I run across the floor to a better position, but Mum has got the carrier and presses it against the wall where I am, so I have no option but to slide into it! 'Yowl!'

'Got her!' yells Mum, closing the door of my carrier, and then she looks a bit guilty. 'You know I don't think I like having to catch her like this. She really doesn't want to come home!'

Well, it is not that I don't want to come home. I'd like her to make up her mind where she wants me – here or there. I think I have made my point.

Minutes later we are back home and I am eating supper before climbing out of the window for a night-time stroll. I make her worry a bit by staying out too long.

By the time we are snuggled up to go to sleep, we are friends again and I am purring. I can't be cross with her for too long.

25th August 2010

Mum is so amused by what she calls my 'tantrum' last night that she writes about it on Pete Wedderburn's (the Telegraph vet's) Facebook page, Pete the Vet. She seems to think it is funny, but he is not so amused. He posts a message back to her, asking if I am OK and not in any sort of distress. And he says he hopes it is a one-off. Mum starts to panic at this and says 'Oh it's just Kimmy.' But she doesn't sound so sure.

We're both rather tired today, as we didn't sleep well. I had strange and very vivid dreams and I made lots of loud grunting noises during the night. I found it hard to settle and a few times I woke Mum. But she gets up and tries to find a reason not to go to yoga and then she goes anyway. I settle down on the bed for a good long nap to catch up on lost zzzzzz. Mum comes back and joins me. I don't know why she exercises when it always makes her so tired. If I was her I would follow my example and eat and sleep all day. I am still gorgeous this way.

Guinness shows up in the evening, but I run away from him, jumping in the window with just seconds to spare before his big, ugly body can follow me into the room – but Mum slams the window hard in his face. You'd think he would be used to this by now?

(Note from Christine – I thought Kimmy's tantrum was quite amusing, as it seemed almost human and in keeping with her 'Countess-like' personality, and was surprised by Pete's reply because it made me realise that maybe he was right and that she was in distress. Sometimes we forget that they are not human and don't have the same emotions as us. Oh, if only we could talk to them...)

26th August 2010

After breakfast – a decent sized one for a change – and going out into the garden for my morning stroll, I am just settling down for the first of my morning naps when Mum does exactly the same as she did the other day: she picks me up and carries my still-sleepy body to the carrier and plonks me in it! I am about to object, but it hardly seems worth it, as I know it will make no difference. I just hope that she isn't taking me to the vet...

Gran arrives in her funny little car and I am put in the back and we drive in the direction of – the vet's! They are chattering away about this and that and ignoring me altogether. After a very short drive, we arrive and I am carried into the busy waiting room. 'Kimmy to get her teeth cleaned,' says Mum to the lady on reception and then adds 'If she needs it …?' The receptionist just nods and tells us to take a seat, and I look around me nervously. There are no dogs this time but a cat looking as miserable as me in a carrier. We stare at each other for a while and I decide not to hiss. There is no real point anyway. Mum and Gran are talking about some stupid woman in the newspaper who picked up a cat she found sitting on a wall and put it in a dustbin. The cat was closed in there for almost a whole day and I am shocked when I hear this. I try to imagine what that would be like. Far worse than being in a carrier I am sure.

The vet's door suddenly opens and Naomi comes out, all smiles as usual when she sees me. 'Kimmy!' she cries. 'And this must be Kimmy's Gran?' she asks Gran, who looks a bit embarrassed, as she hates being called 'Gran.' Naomi has read my latest book and, as Mum carries me in, Naomi tells her how much she's enjoyed it.

'I really feel as if I know you and Kimmy,' she says, and Mum goes that funny red colour – like she does when she lies in the sun for too long – and she tries to tip me out.

'I am sort of hoping,' Mum begins, 'That Kimmy's teeth are OK now. I'd hate to have her taken to the hospital to have them cleaned.'

Naomi nods and holds me firmly, and tips back my head and opens my mouth wide. Ouch… that hurt!

'Oooh,' she says loudly. 'It doesn't look great. Look at all this decay.' Mum peers in and mutters, 'Yes, it does look a bit…' Her voice tails off. Then Naomi is feeling my jaw and she gives another shriek. 'Oh feel this… feel this… This isn't good,' she says.

I am quite alarmed and so is Mum as she presses her hands to my chin and feels a marble-sized hard lump.

'What is it? An abscess? A boil? Something painful?' asks Mum nervously.

'No, nothing like that. Feel how hard it is. This is not good,' Naomi repeats. 'It wasn't here last time, so it has just come up. It's not an infection…'

The words hang there until Mum says slowly, in a squeaky whisper.

'It's not cancer, is it?'

Naomi nods and shakes her head at the same time. And makes notes on her computer. She is speaking very fast now. 'You'll need to bring her in tomorrow. I'll need to get a swab… a biopsy.'

Mum's voice is now very high. 'But you can do something? I mean this isn't… Well, it can be cured?' She gabbles on.

'We'll take a look and see. But there is an operation where we can take away the part of the jaw… half her jaw…'

For once, Mum is silent. She says absolutely nothing, but I am now back in my carrier and I've been placed on a chair. As I strain to listen, the carrier suddenly wobbles and I go downward to the floor with a big crash.

'Kimmmmmy!' shriek Mum and Naomi as they pick me up and place me back on the vet's table.

Naomi tells Mum where and when to bring me – the next day – and Mum nods numbly, muttering now so I can't hear.

We both leave the surgery with the words 'This is not good' ringing in our ears and Mum sits in the waiting room with Gran for some time before she picks me up and takes me back to the car.

Something is wrong and I have no idea what it is.

(Note from Christine – the worst thing I thought would come out of this day was that Kimmy would need to have her teeth cleaned. These types of procedures were never carried out in the local surgery but always at the bigger veterinary hospital about six miles away. I was worried about how she would feel, being separated from me for that time, but had already asked Mum if she would run us there and maybe wait while she had it done. I think I could easily have cancelled this appointment, not realising how important it might be. I had no idea or inkling that Kimmy had this quite sizeable lump under her chin and, when 'cancer' came into the conversation, I felt real terror. I used the words that vets hate to hear: 'I will pay anything to have Kimmy made well. Money is not a problem.' It was true that it wasn't and I would have paid anything, but it is horrible saying the words. It felt as if I was saying, 'I know you will only save her if I offer you lots of money,' which must be such an insult to a vet. I am insured anyway, but had the insurance not covered it, I would have paid – anything. When I carried Kimmy out of the surgery, I was too shocked to move for a while, so after I told Mum, we both sat in numb silence. And I knew it was really bad because the receptionist was looking at the computer screen and reading what it said. She wasn't saying anything to me, which is what they do when they have read something bad and are not sure what to say.

I clung on to the belief that maybe it was something dental or, if worst came to the worst, there was the option of this jaw removal surgery – as horrific as it sounded. Vets are so clever now – they had to be able to do 'something,' didn't they?)

Mum carries me in – far more gently this time – and she doesn't drop me. She releases me from the box and I run off to hide under the bed. There is no way I am coming near her for a while after this. Later on I will probably scratch either the armchair or the rug – possibly both.

She gets on her computer and I can hear her typing frantically. 'Ok, just ignore me,' I think, as I ignore her.

(Note from Christine – I didn't really know what to do with myself when I got back, so I decided to email Pete Wedderburn again and ask his advice. I could hardly remember what Naomi had said and possibly I'd gotten the wrong end of the stick. He would calm me and tell me that she would probably find a badly impacted tooth or an abscess – some sort of easy-to-treat swelling. I Googled 'tumour on the jaw' and found only horrible things that more or less said 'no chance.' I copied what I read and sent it to Pete and awaited his reply.

He got back to me later and didn't really manage to make me feel as good as I'd hoped. He said the article on Google was 'rubbish,' but I wouldn't know what the trouble was until I got the biopsy results in about a week. There was too much guesswork. But he also said the jaw surgery was not as bad as it sounded and was a real option. So Naomi hadn't been wrong then? I scanned the words of his email and read on. He was suggesting that I ask for an x-ray and something called a fine needle aspirate – to see if there were any abnormal cells in the lymph nodes. He finished by saying that it sounded as if we'd probably caught the cancer nice and early. Cancer. He too thought it was cancer. How had this all happened so fast and why hadn't I seen the lump? How could anything like this happen to my perfect cat who had been given the best care and love since I had first got her? How had I missed this? I just couldn't lose her. I couldn't. Why couldn't I make everyone understand this?)

I go out in the garden and get chased by Guinness again. I wonder if he ever gets taken to the vet. He doesn't look like the sort of cat who is made to do anything. It is the perfect end to a not great day. I jump back in through the window and onto Mum's bed. We both sleep badly. And as I drop off I remember: no one said anything about cleaning my teeth.

Autumn

27th September 2010

I wake Mum as usual at around five thirty a.m for my breakfast but she says 'No Kimmy' and turns over and goes back to sleep – except I can see she isn't asleep at all – she is just too lazy to get up and get my breakfast. I try everything I can, purring, nuzzling and licking her hand and walking all over her, but she doesn't budge until much later when she pads out to the kitchen with me in hot pursuit. I go straight to my dish and mew urgently but, to my dismay, she ignores me. 'I'm sorry Kimmy. I can't give you breakfast today,' she says in a slightly high-pitched voice. 'But if you can't eat then neither will I.' Although I can't help thinking it would be a lot better if she ate and let me eat too, I decide to change tactics and ask to go out instead, and moments later I am climbing out of the window into the garden. By the time I come in again she will have my breakfast ready, I tell myself, but instead, when I do haul myself through the window, I am grabbed and put in my carrier with the lid closed firmly. Then I hear her on the phone: 'I've got her Mum,' she is saying, 'And I think we should take her soon and get this over with.'

Get what over with?

Soon I am being carried out of the door to Gran's car, with a sinking heart. Not the vet again! But we drive in a totally different direction from usual and, from my little prison, I can see blue sky, green fields, and I can smell something bad… like my litter tray, only worse. I think we are in the country! We are in the country for a while and then we are in a town with traffic. We pull into a big car park. Mum lifts me gently from the back seat and seems to be concerned, but I am more worried that I haven't had my breakfast and she has *never* not given me breakfast before – *never.* OK, maybe once.

I am carried into a much bigger place that I know is a vet's because it is full of big dogs and they are all barking – at me, I think. Mum places me, in my carrier, on the counter and asks if she can speak to Naomi. A few moments later, Naomi appears and Mum tells her what Pete said and asks for a fine needle aspirate and an x-ray. Then she sits down and frets that she has offended Naomi by telling her what to do. Gran assures her that it is OK and then a woman comes over to us and says 'Kimmy Wilson!' That is me! I am carried into a small room and put on a table while a woman asks Mum lots of questions about me. This was what it was like when my previous Mum took me to Bath Cats and Dogs Home all those years ago. She was asked lots of questions and then she went off and left me. This can't be happening again! Can it?

Mum is crying now and that is a very bad sign because she must be upset about something: is it me? Then, brushing a tear away, she says,

'Goodbye Kimmy – I will see you soon!' And walks off leaving this other woman to carry me from the room to a row of cages – *cages* – where I am lifted from my carrier. I am placed in one but not before I let out a very loud hiss of anger. I don't really know much about what happens next. I remember being lifted out again and then going to sleep – a deep sleep quite unlike the naps I take – and when I wake up, I feel very sore indeed and can taste something nasty and sticky in my mouth – blood. I am bleeding and I feel sleepy still, even though I want to wake up very badly. Hands are stroking me, but they aren't Mum's, so I don't really want them. What happened to me? And why?

I feel myself being carried into the little room where Mum left me and, a few minutes later, Mum appears with Gran. They are both looking at me and I feel myself being lifted upwards into Mum's arms, but I struggle and she puts me back into the horrible cage – so small I can barely stand up or turn round. I try to get out but don't really have the strength and feel so tired still. Then the vet comes in and says some things and Mum is listening very hard, but she keeps asking her to say them again as if she hasn't listened. And then I have a needle stuck in me before someone says 'She can go home now.'

I don't need to be told twice. I am lifted into my carrier – I can't get in fast enough this time. I am carried back to the car, but I am so drowsy: I think I should be scared but feel too sleepy and dazed, and the blood is still oozing through my teeth and out of my mouth. My fur feels all matted and sticky, but I am glad to be with Mum and Gran even though I am so angry with them for having done this to me. Why have they done this?

The journey home seems quicker this time and I am carried in, and the door to my carrier is opened. I am so relieved to be back in a familiar place again. I remember that I haven't eaten and I run to my food bowl and cry angrily to Mum. This time I will not take 'no' for an answer. She puts milk down first and I try to lap it up, but it goes all pink from the blood and I look up at her. *Feed me proper food!* She puts cat food down on a saucer and I eat it hungrily, almost sucking it up, as it hurts a bit – a lot – and it begins to fill my tummy, although the saucer has turned red with blood. I run away into the bedroom and hide under the bed. I can hear her on the phone: 'She's eating, Mum!' I hear her say, but what else did she expect? I have missed at least two meals by now.

Mum keeps coming in and looking at me, but I won't let her touch me. I am very angry and disappointed in her and I can taste more blood coming out of me. Then she's on the phone again to someone and back under the bed, trying to pull me out. 'No you don't!' I yowl as she tries to catch me, and I run into the living room with Mum running after me. I look around desperately and see a window not quite closed. In a flash, I am up on the ledge and I push it hard with my sore face – the gap gets wider. I can squeeze out and run away from here. I haul myself up and am about to jump out, feeling the fresh air on my body. I would run and run and keep running. I can feel Mum's arms closing tightly around me and pulling me hard – far harder than she has ever pulled before. But I pull too and am *so nearly out!* Then I am back in again and the window is closed hard and Mum is pulling me towards a chair and wrapping me in a towel and pushing it hard against my mouth and chin. *It hurts!* She holds me like this. It seems like forever until I struggle and run away, back under the bed, where she can't get me. She comes in and closes the bedroom door. The bedroom door is never closed, as I hate being shut in, but she has shut me in! I am furious. Then I hear the door open again and a saucer of food is pushed under the bed and she gets into the bed. I don't get up beside her as I usually would. A little later, she gets up and opens the bedroom door, as I am crying so much. I run out and leave her. I don't want to be anywhere near her tonight – I want to run away but can't, as all the windows are now closed. So I satisfy myself by rubbing my sticky, bloody face all round the rug and eating what is left of my supper. I think we both sleep badly that night.

(Note from Christine – Not feeding Kimmy was almost the worst part of the day, as she loved her breakfast and always ate well. I had to ignore her pitiful mews. I decided that I would not eat until she did, as I couldn't bear to eat in front of her and I really didn't want to anyway. I let her out for a while, as it was still early and, when she came in, I took the opportunity to grab her and put her in her carrier. I called Mum and asked if she could come a little earlier so we could get on our way to the vet's hospital at Ballyclare, about six miles away.

I asked to speak to Naomi about Pete's suggestions – this fine needle aspirate, and I thought I saw a flicker of irritation on her face, as if I was either stating the obvious or was appearing to tell her what to do, but I hoped she knew that Pete was a friend and that I would be bound to have spoken to him, and also that I was absolutely desperate.

'Do your best for her,' I urged, but felt stupid because I knew that she wouldn't do anything less. I hope she just realised how distressed and upset I was.

I had planned to stay at the vet's all day, but the nurse thought it would be evening before Kimmy could come home and not only is the town a small place to hang around, but neither of us was in the mood to do anything. The vet's waiting room was large and noisy, so we opted to go home and wait for news of the biopsy, but leaving Kimmy there had me crying and I couldn't make the day go fast enough. I went home and cleaned the oven in a desperate attempt to keep busy and not be alone with my thoughts.

The vet's nurse called at midday to say that Kimmy was 'in recovery' and was trying to sit up. 'We will be along straight away!' I said, delighted at the speed of it all.

'No… give us a call around three and we will tell you how she is doing,' said the nurse firmly and I hung up with a heavy heart, before starting some frantic vacuuming – the noise making me miss Naomi's call so I had to call her back.

'It wasn't good,' said Naomi, not beating around the bush. 'The jaw has crumbled and it was a bit of a mess. We may have to consider this jaw surgery to give her a chance.'

I only heard these last words and hung up miserably. I hadn't expected 'good news,' but now that I'd heard it was bad, I was still shocked. How had this happened? How had it got this bad so fast?

Naomi said we could come early to sit with Kimmy until she was ready to go home and we couldn't get there fast enough. I brought a bottle of wine for Naomi and a little note to thank her and I honestly believe I was trying to say to a higher power, 'Look, I'm nice, please let Kimmy be OK,' but I was grateful to Naomi and her kindness. Surely things were not as bad as they sounded and the jaw surgery was still a possibility. Maybe that could happen soon?

Seeing Kimmy all bloody, with her teeth oozing blood

through the gums – shaved around her face and neck and staggering around her crush cage – was yet another very low point and made me realise how serious the operation had been. She had several stitches and seemed to barely know who we were. She looked confused, sleepy and restless and I tried to hold her in my arms, but she struggled too much and clearly wanted to escape and run away. Both the nurse and the vet were telling me things, but none of them made any sense to my baffled brain and thank goodness all the instructions for the medication had been written out for us. Kimmy had pain killers and antibiotics and some mild tranquilisers. The stitches were self-dissolving and I was told if she pulled at them too much she would need to wear one of those awful collars – the lampshades. I was also told to bring her back the following Tuesday to my local clinic for a checkup (Monday was a bank holiday). She was given a final shot of pain-killer and then I was told I could take her home. As the treatment was being covered by our insurance, Petplan, I didn't have to stop at the desk to pay, but even if I had needed to, I might have forgotten; such was my anxiety to get out and get her home. One great thing about insurance is that, not only does it mean the treatment is paid for, but it means that the vet's surgery takes care of it all, so you can make fast exits without having to fumble for credit cards and wait for someone to tell you what is owed. This particular practice took care of it all with Petplan. But I must stress I would willingly have paid any amount of money to have Kimmy saved.

Once safely back home, I got to smile for the first time that day, as Kimmy went straight to her food dish and angrily asked for food. It was just after five p.m – her supper time. I put down milk first, as I wasn't sure if she could manage much else, but she lapped it up and asked for proper cat-food.

Afterwards she ran away from me and hid under the bed. I tried to pour myself some wine and force down the first food of the day but had no real appetite. I wanted to let Kimmy sleep but was upset to see her under the bed rather than on it, where she would normally be, and I hated to see her distress. I crushed half a tranquiliser into some food and took it in to her and she ate it, but the saucer was covered in blood, and when I went in later to check on her the blood was coming out in a fast, steady flow. Alarmed, I called the emergency twenty-four hour service and a vet called me back. He was very kind and told me to hold a towel around her and press hard on the wound until the blood stopped. As she was under the bed I had to try and grab her and pull her out, but she ran from me and into the living room where a bit of a chase began, all adding to my misery. Then, to my horror, I could see her jumping up towards a slightly open window. How had I left a window open? In a flash, she had opened it further and was so nearly out, but with every ounce of my strength I pulled her back in and I felt her pull equally hard. Still I won, and soon she was back in the room and I'd snapped the window closed and had a towel held firmly around her, pressing on the flow of blood. I was feeling absolutely petrified. How had I nearly let her escape? If she had got out in her half-tranquilised, still half-under-anaesthetic-and-very-scared-state, she'd have run and run and I am not sure I would have ever seen her again. The shock of this near disaster – and my stupidity – made me feel physically ill.

I held the towel there for as long as I could before she struggled free, but it seemed to have done the trick. She ran back to the bedroom – under the bed – and I closed her in, while I attempted to clean blood off the carpet. Then I decided to call it a day and I went to join her, but her scraping at the door and crying became too much for me. Kimmy always hated being closed in. So I opened the bedroom door and let her run free around the flat. I fell into a fitful sleep and dreaded the next day.)

28th August 2010

I wake Mum at five thirty as usual and am cross because I want breakfast. She seems pleased for once and gets up straight away, and I eat hungrily, as my mouth feels a bit better and it no longer feels as if I am eating glass. She wants to hug and stroke me, but I pull away, as I still haven't forgiven her, and I go back under the bed, where she leaves me in peace. Mercia, her friend, comes to visit and peers in at me in hiding, but she soon goes away and I spend most of the day avoiding Mum despite all her efforts. I feel a bit better but I am still very sleepy – and very confused.

(Note from Christine – I was so relieved to see her on the bed as usual. wanting food, and even more relieved to see she had cleaned her face and neck completely. How had she managed this? I had expected to have to clean her up and it was so much better that she had done it herself. She looked far more like herself. She ate well but ran back under the bed and ignored me for the rest of the day.

We had dozens of messages on Facebook from her friends all over the world, wishing her well, and it was both comforting and sad to read them all. Her page had been so happy and fun-filled, and now it was full of sadness.

My feelings about the jaw surgery were starting to falter. I had seen the effect of the comparatively minor biopsy and the distress it had caused her. I'd seen her bloody face and shaved body and felt that I couldn't put her through an operation that would take half her jaw away. If she hated me now, how would she feel after the much bigger operation? Surely I could spare us that. I would willingly have undergone the surgery for her if it was in any way possible, but it wasn't, and I emailed Pete to say as much. He emailed straight back to say I should wait for the biopsy results and not jump the gun. He also pointed out that eighty-six percent of cat owners who had had the operation were 'glad' they did. So I took some hope in the possibility that perhaps the biopsy results – to be received within five days – would be encouraging or that the surgery would be offered and that I would be one of the lucky eighty-six percent. We still had options and, in this whole dreadful scenario, options were what we needed.

29th August 2010

I wake up feeling better and look at Mum, sleeping fitfully, and suddenly I forgive her. I know that she has been feeling bad and, as I now feel so much better, it is easier to love her again. I climb into the bed and we spend a few hours just napping – me purring beside her. Later Gran comes round and everyone is so much happier. I am allowed to go out and I walk round the garden. It all looks good. My life is OK again.

(Note from Christine – Today was one of our best days and I felt so pathetically grateful. Kimmy woke me purring and we snuggled together for most of the morning, both tired from the past few days, before getting up to see Mum and to buy papers, which I took back to bed. The best bits of my last few years have all been spent snuggling in bed with Kimmy pushed in close to my side. She looked more like her old self; her wound was clean and looked less raw. It was a good day, the first for a while and, while we dozed, I allowed myself to feel optimistic. I fell asleep, praying that God would give us longer together.

30th August 2010
(Note from Christine – It was a bank holiday and I felt somehow 'safe'. I knew that no bad news would come today and no one could 'touch us' in any way. Had it not been a holiday I would have spent the day sitting by the phone in case the results came back earlier than expected. I found myself wishing that this holiday would go on forever.

I updated everyone on Kimmy's Facebook page and read the many new messages: Jan, Debby, Marketa (she works for cancer research so offered a good deal of advice), Etta... so many people all sending concerned messages. I wanted to send them back good news.

If also occurred to me that, just a few weeks' ago, I was fretting about the stubborn half stone I had put on and couldn't lose, but now, having not eaten for about four or five days, my clothes felt loose and my face looked pinched. Sometimes we need to be careful what we wish for.)

31st August 2010

I'm feeling much better now but am amazed when, shortly after giving me breakfast, Mum shoves me into my carrier once more and puts me in the back of the car.

This can't be happening – can it? We are off to the vet again!

This time it is the local vet's, so not so far to go. I am really cross about it though, and we have to wait ages too. I'd have happily waited even longer – and not seen her at all – but at last I hear my name being called. 'Kimmy!' It isn't nice Naomi but a different vet – another lady – and I am not having any of it this time. I hiss at her and try to lash out with my paw. I also refuse to come out of the carrier until gravity gets the better of me. Then I try to leg it, but Mum catches me and puts me on the table. The lady vet prods at my mouth and neck and says lots of things very, very fast. Then quick as a flash we are out

Kimmy on tissue paper

again and heading home. That wasn't so bad after all.

I am thrilled with all the food I am getting. Mum seems to feed me every time I so much as look at my plate – and she gives me a yummy choice too: salmon, tuna and all sorts of packet cat food. Clearly the diet is off and I am glad of that as I tuck into my fourth meal of the day. I am able to go out as well and have a really good sniff around. She is on her computer a lot these days too, but she is also at home a good deal more. She used to go out but now she spends all her time with me. I like that. The nasty stitches in my mouth are really starting to annoy me now and I try to pull at them, but it hurts when I get my claw caught in them, and Mum gets all upset and has to try and untangle my paw from the stitch. Ouch!

To celebrate nothing bad happening today I decide to sit on a piece of tissue paper all afternoon. It is bliss.

(Note from Christine – I wanted the bank holiday to go on forever, but today it was back to business and I had to take Kimmy to the vet to have a checkup. We didn't see Naomi, as she was at the other surgery and it felt too far to take Kimmy, so we saw Kirstin instead. Kirsten, like Naomi, has a reputation for being an excellent vet and is often the first choice for those who want 'the best,' (actually they are all good). She talked very fast to us as she looked at Kimmy, (who was quite clearly distressed this time) and much of what she said was a bit lost on me, although I did understand certain things. She was implying that Naomi suspected Kimmy's cancer could turn out to be quite aggressive and that surgery might not be an option. I hadn't really realised this so I found myself saying 'So we will be lucky to be offered the surgery?'

'Well let's wait and see,' said Kirstin, but she was nodding.

I was also thinking of something else she had said earlier – something about 'the signs' – and there was an unspoken question: hadn't I noticed anything? Well had I? Yes, it is true that I had noticed her face was a slightly different shape. I couldn't put my finger on it – it was as if her chin were slightly pointier, but as she had just lost a fair amount of weight, I had wrongly assumed that the weight loss had changed her face shape a bit, as it does with us all. I thought she had lost neck fat, which made her face look even prettier than usual. The weight loss I had been so thrilled with: I was sure it had been down to her increased exercise and dieting, but now I had to ask – was it the cancer? I had noticed a little bit of dribble on her chin, but I had put it down to possibly her teeth needing a clean, which was why I'd brought her in to see Naomi in the first place. Her little tongue being out more than usual? Yes, I had noticed that too but I didn't make a connection between any of these things. Until now. You just don't think, 'Oh my cat is dribbling a bit – it must be cancer.' She seemed so well, ate well and enjoyed life enormously. I felt dreadful when I thought more about this. My cat had had cancer, possibly for some weeks, and I hadn't noticed. Every night I would stroke her and often I would brush her. She would sleep beside me. I was sure I knew every inch of her body, but I had missed something important – a marble-sized lump on her chin. That realisation was very hard to take as I tried to work out if it could have made a difference. I would never ignore anything like this again – although it was probably too late and I wouldn't get a chance.

I didn't really expect any results that day and, when we got to six o'clock, I was beginning to feel 'safe' from anything more worrying than what we had already heard. So when the phone rang at six thirty, I was surprised to find it was Naomi.

She asked how Kimmy was and chatted in a very friendly way and made a joke about Kimmy not liking vets anymore. I started to relax. This was just a social phone call. She couldn't have bad news if she was joking like this.

'I've got some results,' she said and my heart froze.

'It looks as if she might have a lymphoma, which is a far easier cancer to treat. We can treat it with chemo,' she was saying. I struggled to take this in.

'No surgery then?'

'No. We can do it with chemo.'

A ton of weight dropped off my shoulders.

'Would the chemo be bad?'

'No, not at all. But I am waiting to hear from the Vet School in Edinburgh. I'll get back to you and we might be able to get Kimmy started this week.'

Oh, the relief. I could have cried with joy. All my prayers had been answered. Kimmy had a sort of cancer that could be treated without surgery and she was going to be OK. I asked Naomi to email the results to Pete and thanked her profusely. Then I got on the phone and told as many people as possible and the rest heard by email.

The timing of the news was especially good, as I had planned to go to Bath that weekend to do a book signing at the Bath Cats and Dogs Open Day for "Kimmy's Irish Diary." I would just be away one night and, as Pete Wedderburn was going to be a guest speaker and judge too, it would be good to go and see him. I had been unsure if it would be OK to go, with everything up in the air, but now it looked more likely. I could go and perhaps Kimmy could start her chemo the following week? After all the stress and pressure of the past days, this would be a real tonic for me.

And as if the day couldn't get any better, I went onto Kimmy's Facebook page and found a message from Ann. We had fallen out a few months before over something stupid and I was so relieved to hear from her. Ann is a very funny woman but she is also very sensitive and I adore her two cats, Pancho and Cisco. On United Cats, Ann with the help of Supurr Cisco, runs The League of Supercat Heroes, a virtual club for all our cats to meet, robed in photo-shopped capes, and do 'missions'. They (virtually) fly to places that have had disasters, to rescue cats in distress, search for lost pets, and keep vigil by sick cats. Perhaps their most important role was to meet with the spirit of a recently departed cat and fly to Rainbow Bridge, where they would be met by other cats recently or not so recently departed. It may all sound like total madness but in fact it wasn't. The Rainbow Bridge escorts, although terribly poignant, were of huge help to bereaved pet parents struggling to come to terms with sudden loss or loss of hope after illness. Cats – or any pets for that matter – do not get the funerals that humans get and which provide so much comfort in a dark hour – being surrounded by friends saying lovely things about the departed. One of Kimmy's first missions had been a vigil for Ann's very sick Kittibits, who was clinging to life, and it was terribly sad. We even threw a virtual wake for 'Bits, after he succumbed, to bring a little happiness back. Ann's LOSCH did and still does untold good work for the grieving and also brings many smiles to hundreds of adoring pet lovers. (www.UnitedCats.com/ Leagueofsupercatheroes)

I told her how pleased I was and went to bed finally, and slept well for the first time in ages.)

1st September 2010

You will never guess what happened this morning? I had breakfast and was sitting on the bed looking at a crack in the curtain – and then I saw it – a terrible sight. It was Guinness looking in at me – his big black face staring. I yowled loudly and growled too. Mum was asleep but not anymore! She woke with a start and jumped out of bed. Whipping back the curtain, she saw him there. The horrible Guinness! I ran from the room so I didn't have to see him anymore and Mum pulled the curtains tightly shut.

He really is a terrible pest. Mum goes off to tell my fans about it on Facebook and she reads something from Pete Wedderburn that seems to upset her, but apart from that, our day is OK. Mum stays in with me and spends a lot of her time at her computer. I do a lot of eating and sleeping – my two favourite things.

(Note from Christine – I felt very tired when I woke up because, for some reason, this new 'good news' hadn't properly sunk in, although I did manage to eat some breakfast and decided to go to yoga. But first I checked my email...Pete had emailed me to say that he had seen Kimmy's results and that there was 'some misunderstanding'. They were the 'fine aspirate results' and not the biopsy results. I would still have to wait for those.

I immediately felt sick and quickly emailed back. 'But Naomi was talking about chemo now and hadn't mentioned that these were anything other than 'the results'. What did this mean?

Pete replied very quickly to say that the fine aspirate results – a sample taken from the lymph node – were just an indicator of whether cancer cells were present and were often a very fair sign of what the biopsy would say but that I would still have to wait for those. Oh no... once again I was waiting for possibly bad news. Quickly I thought back to what Naomi had said. She'd said she had 'some' results for me and I had assumed they were 'the results'. But now I was not out of the woods and would have to play the waiting game again.

With a sinking heart, I had to un-tell everyone the 'good' news and try and explain that I had jumped the gun a bit and that we still had to wait for the biopsy results which would probably come Thursday or Friday at the latest.

I went online to see what the Internet said about fine needle aspirate.

"Sometimes suspicious tissues are aspirated with needles to harvest cells for diagnostic purposes. It is particularly helpful to aspirate an enlarged lymph node or swelling to see if there is a tumour. Aspiration is not as accurate as biopsy but is less invasive and may not require anaesthesia depending on the location of the suspected tumour. Fine needle aspiration is a test your vet may recommend."

It also said:

'Regular teeth cleaning is important for all pets. In pets, regular dental care at the vet's office may mean early tumour detection."

I didn't go out all day but waited by the phone – just in case Naomi rang. Did this mean that the chemo was no longer an option? Was the dreadful jaw surgery back on the agenda again and would I be able to go to Bath that weekend as planned? Or should I be letting people know I couldn't come? The hotel would charge me if I didn't let them know in time and my friends were making plans to see me. Laura Craig Gray was travelling from Oxford and another friend from London, and Bath Cats and Dogs Home were expecting me to do a book signing for "Kimmy's Irish Diary." With a shaking hand I alerted my friends to the possibility of my not coming and continued what was now becoming a habit: I waited for the phone to ring.)

2nd September 2010

(Note from Christine – my mother had phoned to suggest coming round to sit with Kimmy for an hour or so while I went out. She knew I had barely left the flat for about a week while waiting for calls from the vet about test results, and she was keen to give me a break. For a moment I was tempted – very tempted – as I felt like a pressure cooker waiting to blow. But then I realised that, for Mum, this had been nearly as bad. She was also very stressed and upset so, with a deep breath, I devised a plan.

'Mum, let's go out together for an hour or so. Naomi has a clinic up the road from – ten to eleven, so she won't phone me then and I doubt she will phone before eleven thirty, as she has to get back to Ballyclare after. If we go out and are back by then – and I have my mobile phone with me – I am

sure we will be OK. She may not phone till much later in the day anyway.'

I could hear the relief in Mum's voice. A little trip to Marks and Spencer and maybe a cup of coffee would do us both good. So as arranged, Mum turned up at ten and off we went. We had coffee, but I began to feel anxious, looking at my phone every few minutes. Mum could see my tense face and suggested we do our shopping and get home. I just threw a few items into my basket in the food-hall, hardly paying any attention to what I bought, but Mum took a little longer. Two shoppers are always slower than one and, as I watched her fumbling for her bag and her change, I stood nearby, silently saying the words 'hurry up'. We got home and I dashed inside to pick up the phone – it was giving the burring sound that told me I had a message and, with a sinking heart, I realised who it was from.

Naomi had called just five minutes before to say that she had Kimmy's biopsy results and needed to discuss them with me. She said she was leaving at two and would try to get back to me before then. I felt my heart freeze and my face went clammy as I listened again to the message. This had to be bad news. If it was good, she'd have said or she'd have called me on my mobile phone, so with a shaking hand, I dialled her number and learned she was consulting, so I left a message for her to call me back. For well over an hour, I paced the floor, willing her to ring and at last she did.

'It's not good,' she said, plunging me into deeper despair. There are cancer cells and, to be honest, I am not sure what to do next... I don't think the operation... but I will take some advice from the Veterinary College in Edinburgh.' She also asked if I would be prepared to take her there, (to Edinburgh)

if necessary. 'Yes,' I said emphatically. It was all I could take in really after 'It's not good'. Afterwards I sank into an armchair before pulling myself together to go and cancel my hotel room in Bath and tell people I wouldn't be able to come. I also emailed Pete, to ask his advice, and then settled down for another full afternoon of waiting for more news – only this time my Internet broadband signal kept going and I wanted to leave my landline free in case news came.

Pete emailed me in the evening to say he had received the biopsy results (forwarded to him by Naomi's surgery) and was going to look at them and get back to me. I felt a spark of hope. He would see something and know what to do. Maybe I could take Kimmy to him – to his surgery and he could save her? I just knew he would know what to do.

Pete's reply came fast and was short: 'Can I phone you? What is your number?'

With a shaking hand, I typed it out and waited for his call.

I had never heard his voice before and it sounded soft and gentle. I felt immediately reassured – but not for long.

'I've seen the results,' he said, 'and they are very clear.'

I held my breath and said nothing as I sank into the sofa.

'Do you want me to explain them to you?'

'No. Just cut to the quick,' I said, knowing my brain was running on a very low battery.

'I will put it in layman's terms?'

'Ok,' I said miserably.

He went on to explain gently that Kimmy had a very bad type of cancer – one of the worst a cat could get – and that surgery wouldn't remove it, as there would not be enough healthy flesh left, after the cancer was cut out, to give the margin that was required to make the surgery a success. These margins are essential otherwise the cancer can't be fully removed. He explained that the jaw surgery was a really nasty operation requiring feeding tubes to be fitted and that it was distressing for a cat. It would only be worth doing if there was a good chance of success and, in this case, there wasn't. If I insisted on the operation, I would be doing it simply for myself and not for Kimmy's best interests.

That was another rug pulled from under me. 'What about chemo?' I asked hopefully.

'No chemo... no radiotherapy. I'm sorry,' he said, breaking my heart.

I had no options now at all.

'How long?' I whispered, the tears beginning to come.

Pete gave a long sigh. 'It's hard to say, but the average length of time is seven months, based on cats who live just over a year and those who don't make a month.'

It sounded so stark. Kimmy had just seven months to live. Just seven months and possibly less.

Desperately I clung to a straw. 'What about another vet... an older one. Naomi is young and maybe hasn't seen this before. How could she know all this? A different vet – the one who looked after our pets as a child. He was still around and he's far older... far more experienced?'

Pete cut me off. 'Naomi has done everything just right, Christine. First of all, she found the tumour, knowing to look out for it, and then she did the biopsy straight away and she couldn't have done anything more.' Of course, I knew he was right. Naomi was my vet of choice and I liked her and had heard from everyone how good she was, and hadn't Kirstin, the other very good vet, agreed with her? And Pete too... and the labs in Edinburgh? Where else was there to go?

Pete's voice was even more gentle. 'Christine, you always knew you would lose Kimmy one day and that that day would come. Well, it has just come a little sooner than you expected. You would have to face this one day and it is never easy.'

This made sense, of course, except for one major flaw. I never thought I would lose Kimmy. She seemed invincible to me. She had survived being left by her first Mum at Bath Cats and Dogs Home, after having a loving home for ten years. She had survived living by one of Bath's busiest roads – never venturing near it. She had travelled with me from Bath to Northern Ireland. She had returned to our rented flat that terrible first day when we had moved in and she had escaped. She had not lost weight, even while on a diet, and somehow she always gave me the impression she would go on and on like the Queen Mother. Like Countess Kimmy. She had always seemed in robust health. I had never faced up to losing her. But now I would have to.

I thanked him and hung up and I honestly don't know what I did after that. I think I went to bed and tried to sleep away the shock. My last thoughts were of how kind Pete had been to us and what an extraordinary cat Kimmy was to have attracted such a person.)

Mum's been funny all day and hardly looks at me. She seems very upset so, when she comes to bed, I make sure to give her some extra special Kimmy-love and I snuggle beside her with my very best, deepest purr and head butts... Is something wrong? I decide to stare at her until I can work it out.

3rd September 2010

(Note from Christine – I must have slept – I don't know how – because I woke up with Kimmy on my chest, staring into my eyes, and I felt a profound sense of relief that she was still here and, just for a second, I wondered if I had dreamt it all, but it came flooding back. A cup of strong coffee later and I was starting to feel slightly more positive. Kimmy could live for six or seven months – possibly as long as a year. That was a long time for a cat – more like three to seven years for us humans – and she wouldn't have to have that dreadful operation or any more trips to the vet. Maybe as bad as this was, it wasn't as bad as it had seemed last night. I even felt as if I could go to Bath. The hotel was charging me for the room anyway, as I'd tried to cancel too late and the flight was booked. It was just for one night and the break would do me good. Kimmy had recovered from the biopsy and would be fine at Mum's or here with Karyn and Fred looking after her. I'd be back before she noticed and it would be the last time I would leave her now for whatever time she had left. It would be good to fulfil my obligation at Bath Cats and Dogs Home and to meet Pete Wedderburn after all the help he'd given me. I would be with close friends so they would be a comfort. I emailed everyone to let them know I was coming.

The phone rang and I answered it immediately. It was Naomi.

'I've spoken to Edinburgh,' she said. 'And they really don't think radiotherapy or chemo would help...' Her voice sounded nervous.

'It's OK,' I said, with more calmness than I believed possible. I didn't want to hear the whole 'non options' again, so I told her

I had spoken to Pete the night before.

There was a silence for a moment and she reiterated that the operation was no longer an option. Then she dealt the death blow.

'I think the fact that this cancer has grown so fast in such a short space of time, we could be looking at weeks – maybe two.'

I froze on the spot and couldn't hear any more. No one had said that yet. No one had said she may just have weeks – or days to live. Was this some sick joke? Why was it that the news just kept getting worse and worse? Numbly I put down the phone and, with shaking hands, emailed everyone to say I wouldn't be coming to Bath at all now.

The phone rang and it was Pete. He sounded concerned.

'I've just been talking to Naomi,' he said.

'Oh?'

'There is something you didn't tell me.'

I searched my muddled, shocked brain for anything I hadn't said a dozen times over.

'You didn't tell me you'd been in to see her a month before and the lump wasn't there then. You didn't say that Kimmy had been dribbling a bit...'

'Hadn't I? Had I told Naomi that? I suppose I had. My mind flashed back to 22nd July when I had been so thrilled about Kimmy's weight loss and I'd noticed that Naomi didn't quite share my joy and was writing more on her computer than usual. I had assumed she maybe hadn't fully realised what an achievement it was for Kimmy to lose weight after trying for so long. I'd forgotten to mention the dribbling to Pete.

'Dribbling wouldn't be normal for a cat that just needed

her teeth cleaning. But even if she'd done a biopsy then, which wouldn't have been possible, it would still have been too late.'

Pete sounded more serious than he had last night. 'Naomi checked her jaw very carefully that time and felt nothing, yet within a very short time, a tumour had appeared. So I'd have to agree that it could just be weeks. I am so sorry. But at least you know the very worst you can know now. The not knowing is the worst. There is nothing else.'

No indeed. How much worse could it be?

I replaced the phone in a daze and felt a smattering of sympathy for Pete. I hadn't told him something important and he'd been kind enough to speak to Naomi on the phone. It must have been awkward for him when he learned that there was something important he didn't know. I'd made a real mess of this whole situation.

Mum came round and I told her the terrible, revised news and we sat in stunned silence for a long time while I tried to make sense of it all. In just over a week, I'd gone from owning a seemingly healthy cat in need of teeth-cleaning, through possibly having to have a horrible operation or chemo, to having just two weeks to live.

I went online to try and find some more information and I found this.

Oral Squamous Cell Carcinoma (Feline)

The squamous cell carcinoma is not only the most common oral malignancy in cats; it has one of the poorest outcomes. In most cases, the goal is to minimise infection and pain until the tumour has advanced to a state where comfortable eating and/

or breathing is not possible. The tumour is treatable only if detected early in its course.

The average age for diagnosis is 12.5 (which is about the age Kimmy was) and the risk is greater in households that smoke. (I didn't smoke but had no idea if her previous owner had.) It also gave advice on how to check a cat's mouth, but of course that was all too late for me. I can only guess that I had missed a good many symptoms – possibly because we had moved three times in the past year and I'd been distracted? It went on to say (too late for me):

Get comfortable looking in your cat's mouth.
Where to Look
The squamous cell carcinoma often grows from the gums surrounding the teeth or under the tongue. To look under a cat's tongue, press your thumb upward from under the chin (in the soft area between the lower jaw bones). This will raise the base of the tongue upward; when the cat's mouth is open, it's easy to see the root of the tongue. Become familiar with the symmetry and contour of your cat's jaws, both upper and lower.

I wanted to dive under the duvet and not come out again, but instead I got Mum to drive me to the vet's to get more of Kimmy's painkillers, as we were now opting for palliative care – to relieve the pain but not to subject her to further operations. At least Naomi had ordered me a big bottle of the pain relief (Metacam), so she thought Kimmy may have time to use a whole bottle and wasn't giving me a teeny tiddly one that might just last days. I could barely speak to the receptionist for tears and asked her to take Kimmy off the Fat Club register. That was the last thing I needed – a reminder in a few months to bring her in to get weighed. I took the medication and fled back to the car. I asked Mum not to let anyone visit me, as I wanted time alone. I knew everyone would say, with the greatest of intentions, that they knew how I felt, but somehow I had to come to terms with the fact that I had no idea how I felt at all. I felt shocked, upset and tearful and a little angry, but I also knew that this was just the tip of the iceberg. It hadn't fully sunk in and it could be days before I could talk about it. I needed time to think it all through. When I'd lost my father four years before, it had been terribly painful but he had been ill for so long that I'd also had a sense of relief mixed in with my sorrow. He was a very old man who was ready to go and who understood, more or less, what was happening to him. How could Kimmy understand any of this?)

I stare at Mum for ages until she wakes up. I really want her to feed me and staring helps, as eventually she does open her eyes. She smells a bit whiffy and I think she's had some of that fruity stuff that she sometimes drinks, which makes her all silly, although I don't remember her being silly last night.

She spends ages on the phone and at her Internet, ignoring me entirely, so I stay under the bed until Gran comes round and then I come into the room and allow her to play with me and one of my toys – the one on a fishing rod. It is great fun but I wonder why they haven't done this with me before. Why now? They both look very upset and I hope I haven't done anything to upset them so I roll over and show them my tummy and that seems to make them laugh. Then I see Mum brush a tear from her eyes. Something is definitely up and I have no idea what. I hope neither of them is sick. I would hate that.

Later on something really upsetting happens. I am cleaning my face with my paw and my claw gets caught in one of those annoying stitches at the side of my mouth. I pull at it and... ouch! It really hurts. But I can't get my claw out and the more I pull, the more it hurts. Mum comes over and gently pulls my claw away. The pain goes away but it has scared me.

4th September 2010

I sleep as close to Mum as I can, sensing that she is unhappy about something and, when she wakes up, I purr at her. I always love waking up near her, as I feel loved and safe then. A little bit of sunshine is streaming in through the curtains and I really want to go out, but I am worried about Mum so I don't ask her for anything – for food or for the window to be opened – I just stay there beside her, pressed in as close as I can. I have of course already had one breakfast at five thirty and persuaded Mum to let me out of a window so have already done the tour of my domain and taken it all in. Finally Mum gets up and, soon after, I hear her on her computer tap tapping away as she does so much now. I like to watch her while she is tapping at her keyboard. Sometimes she can see me and looks down and smiles but often she doesn't know I am watching her working away. We cats love to watch our humans work. I spend most of the rest of the day just trying to be a good cat and offer her as much support as I can. She looks so sad that I am still worried something is seriously wrong. Gran comes round later and she and Mum chat for ages and I think I can hear Mum crying so I slope off under the bed. All this emotional stuff is hard for a cat to take.

(Note from Christine – I woke without any hope at all. For the past few weeks I had always had some hope. Maybe the lump wouldn't be cancer; maybe it would be benign; possibly an operation or chemo could cure her, and finally maybe six months could stretch to a year. But now there wasn't anything at all to latch onto. I could feel Kimmy's warm, little body beside me and I felt her purring and suddenly realised that she was still alive. I still had her. She was my hope. Jumping out of bed, I emailed Naomi to say that there had to be something she could do for Kimmy. Surely with all the advances of veterinary medicine they could think of some long shot – anything at all. Then I emailed Pete who was off to Bath that day for the Open Day that I wasn't able to attend. He replied with an interesting idea. 'You should write about all this,' he said. 'No one has ever really explained what this is like from a cat and an owner's perspective.' I looked in horror at what he had written. I was far too stressed to write right now and would anyone want to read it? But the idea slowly began to make sense. I was going to be home a good deal over the next few weeks and had to have something to do – and I was supposed to be a writer after all. Maybe it would help? But I banished the thought with the arrival of a package from Israel. Debby Rodrig, one of my friends off United Cats – or rather one of Kimmy's friends really – had sent me a gorgeous home-made yoga bag, a beautiful necklace and a letter that made me cry. In it she talked about how much she had enjoyed reading Kimmy's Diaries and she said that she hoped Kimmy would get well soon, as she was so loved. This surely had to be a sign?

Debby's kindness moved me so much on such a black day that I resolved to do what Pete had suggested; I would write another Kimmy Diary bringing her story up to date. If just one person went and had a minor-looking symptom checked out in their pet, or bought pet insurance – so important if your cat suddenly gets ill and you can't afford the vet's bills – I would feel it had been worth it. I needed a project and this could be it. Watching my mother play with Kimmy and her fishing line toy brought tears to my eyes again and I prayed and prayed that Kimmy would be well again or allowed to live for longer than just a few weeks.

My friend Karyn phoned later, as she'd been away, and I was so relieved to speak to her. She had a cat Flossie, also living with cancer, and I knew that Karyn understood exactly what this was like. I found a lot of comfort in what she said. I even agreed to meet her for a drink the following night. I spent the rest of the evening slumped in front of my television in my 'perfect for Kimmy' flat, staring mindlessly at the screen. Needless to say, I slept badly.)

5th September 2010

Waking up next to Mum is extra nice today, as she doesn't leap out of bed but stays with me for ages, stroking my head and ears so I purr and purr and feel so cosy, but eventually she gets up and I do too. I busy myself with cat-stuff – cleaning my face (why do I get so much extra dribble?) and a gentle walk around the garden to see what's what. I jump back in the window and am just settling myself down for a good nap when Mum swoops down on me and, in a split second, I am in my carrier – not the little one I go to the vet in, but the huge one she used to bring me here from Bath. Where am I going and is it far? I feel myself being carried to Gran's car and have a quick panic.

Not the vet *again*? But to my great relief, we are only going down the road to where Gran and her cat, Uncle Jamie, live. Once there, the door to my carrier is opened and, without delay, I run towards the back doors to the garden and wait to be let out. Mum doesn't disappoint, as she knows how much I love that lovely big garden with a wall all round it and interesting flower beds.

It has rained that morning so the smells are really good and I can see Mum and Gran watching me from the window, but I ignore them until I smell something different – Jamie. The silly cat has hunkered down, so he is flat on his tummy and is crawling along the grass towards me. Did he really think I wouldn't see him? I decide to ignore him and pretend he isn't there and continue to sniff around. I can see he has changed tactics now and, instead of coming straight towards me, he has diverted himself towards a flower bed so he can sneak up behind me. As if!

With one swipe of my paw and a warning hiss, he runs back inside to his mum and I continue with the job in hand: seeking out the source of every good smell and doing my business in my favourite place by the big plant pot. I run inside a few times but just for a snack – Mum has put out saucers of chicken for me and I eat them hungrily, polishing off Jamie's share before going out again and again.

Mum and Gran seem to have settled down to watch something on that box of theirs – we have one too – and I wander in a few times to see what they are doing, but I am happy to have the freedom of a big private garden. This really is heaven for a cat like me.

Jamie seems to have given up trying to annoy me – or so

I think until I catch him trying to climb *into* my carrier, like he did the other day. I mean how stupid is that? Not since he tried to get out of the letterbox, thinking it was a cat-flap (and he doesn't have one), has a cat been so stupid. I want to sneak up behind him and close it after him but I don't. I just hiss as loud as I can and he hears this and runs upstairs to hide. Then I tuck my paws in under me and settle down for a nap – I have missed my morning one.

It is a pretty good day and I am cross when Mum picks me up and puts me back in the now Jamie-smelling box and takes me home. I like going to Gran's – every cat should have a big, safe garden to play in.

Mum goes out later and I miss her. We've had such a good day and I feel a bit lonely without her, but she comes back looking wobbly just when I am starting to worry. I peep my face around the door as she wobbles in and she goes all gooey. 'Oh, Kimmy you are so sweet when you do that.' I used to do it in Bath by peeping round the top of the staircase down into the hall. This time I just have to make do with the bedroom door.

Oh, whatever... I am just glad she is back in time to give me a late supper, and soon we are snuggled up together just like we were at the start of the day.

6th September 2010

(*Note from Christine – Kimmy and I slept late today and yet again I was thankful for the fact that I worked from home and didn't have to leave her to go off to some office to work for eight hours. I would have been no good to any employer at that moment.*

For the past few days I had allowed my emotional side to take over and had been tearful and very emotional but today I put my 'heart' to one side and tried to act with my head. I did a long email to both Pete Wedderburn and Naomi, saying that I was opting for palliative care but needed to know what it entailed and what would happen now. I had to 'know' what lay ahead. At some point I would have to make the heart-breaking decision to have Kimmy put to sleep (my heart trembled for a moment but I allowed my 'head' to keep typing). How would this happen – at the surgery or at home? And if it was necessary – which would be quicker? I had a nightmare vision of watching my beloved cat in pain and having to wait all day for a home visit. I also asked about cremation (the tears were falling) and would I be sure to get my own cat's ashes back and not some other cat's. I asked a practical question about the pain medication – would I need to increase that? I pointed out that Kimmy had had some diarrhoea that morning – did that mean she needed more painkillers? (I had no idea if she was even in pain.) And finally I said I would want a post mortem only if it would help another cat with the same condition. I read and reread it – the tears dripping off my chin – and hit 'send'. Pete, bless him, replied almost immediately.

Hi Christine (copying this to Naomi) probably best to let Naomi answer these questions, but I thought I'd just give you some feedback of my own....Palliative care – my dictionary says "that which lessens pain or gives temporary relief" So in other words, Kimmy can't be cured but she can be given relief from the symptoms of cancer. In practice, this mostly means Metacam drops – and Naomi

will advise you on dosage, although what you're giving sounds right. Other types of pain relief sometimes cause side effects like vomiting or dullness, so you may not be recommended to go there I don't think this is necessarily a painful cancer anyway – more of an "odd" feeling in her mouth, perhaps a strange taste, and as time goes by, an awareness that it "feels" odd because of the swelling of her jaw. Eventually she may stop eating just because it feels so odd. Not sure how much pain there is with it all – it can be hard to tell. When do you make The Decision? I think it will be obvious. For me, it's when an animal stops eating for more than two days. Often they may be bright still so it's not easy, but when there's a terminal diagnosis, and they stop eating, you know that it'd just be another couple of days from then till things get much worse, so it seems right to stop things before that happens. So as long as Kimmy is eating, there's no big hurry at all. Also, no need to organise in advance, I don't think. I suspect she's unlikely to have a sudden big painful crisis (like the unfortunate stitch episode) – it's more likely to be a slower, more chronic situation, so you'll have a window of a day or two, which I hope Naomi can fit in without organising way in advance. Couple of other things – I don't think a post mortem would be likely to be of huge assistance to other cats, but it's kind of you to offer the thought. Her particular illness is already well studied. And when she's cremated, her ashes are definitely HER ashes – the pet crematorium has systems in place to ensure this. You'll probably have a choice of what type of container you'd like them to be brought back in, and again, talk to Naomi

**about this. Hope this all makes sense and do keep in touch
as things progress in the coming weeks....**

All the best

Pete

*I read and reread Pete's email with a mounting sense of
gratitude. Now I felt I was dealing the practical side of this
terrible illness and surely 'knowing' all that lay ahead was
better than the agony of not knowing.*

*Naomi phoned a little later and had picked up on the comment
about diarrhoea. She was worried that Kimmy may be one of
the tiny per cent of cats who can't take Metacam (the pain-
relief) and my heart sank for the nth time in just a few weeks.
Was this going to be yet another blow? If she couldn't take pain
relief then she was not going to be able to have palliative care
at all. But in a flash, I remembered that I had given her milk a
few times recently, which I wouldn't normally do, as I know it
doesn't agree with a cat's stomach – but I had done it because I
thought, with her surgery, eating proper food might be difficult
(it wasn't). I told Naomi and she confirmed this would be the
reason. What a relief! She suggested I give Kimmy Whiskas
milk instead – a milk designed for cats.*

*'You could bring her in to see me – say, next Thursday,' she
suggested and I agreed with a heavy heart. I sort of 'knew'
that, this being ten days away, that was possibly all the time
that Kimmy had left and maybe the appointment would mark
the day that I would have to make the 'decision'. But at least
we had a date to work towards and I wouldn't have to book
something in a panic.*

With all the practical stuff done I went to check on Kimmy, sleeping soundly on the soft blanket on my bed. She looked so peaceful and was so deeply asleep that for a second I feared the worst, but I could see her little chest rising and falling and I thanked God again. I wasn't ready to lose her yet – but the question was – would I ever be? One thing I did know was that I was going to make whatever time Kimmy had left the best time possible. She was going to be spoiled rotten!)

7th September 2010

There is nothing nicer than a dawn breakfast and a walk in the garden.

Normally Mum shoos me away and pulls the duvet over her head, but today she gets up and gives me a nice plateful. Then even more amazingly, she opens the window so I can go out!

It is still quite dark but about to become daylight so I run about looking at everything – the half-built houses and the gardens next door and then, as it is chilly, I begin to feel a bit cold. There is something really special about this time of day and most cats will tell you that an hour of running around this early is worth two later on. I jump back in again and Mum slams the window shut. I sit on the window ledge staring out – this is nearly as good as actually being out, as I can see everything but be lovely and warm indoors. Then suddenly my gaze darkens and all I can see is a big black thing staring in at me. Guinness – the horrible Guinness – is sitting right on the other side of the glass just inches away.

I arch my back and hiss and growl as loudly as I can and Mum comes flying into the room yelling 'Kimmy, are you OK?' She sees what I see and frowns. 'Kimmy, the window is closed!' Quickly she pulls the curtains and hides the evil Guinness from view, and I run off under the bed, although we can still see his silhouette through the curtain and know he's there.

'It's still only six a.m,' moans Mum, climbing back into bed. A moment later she is asleep again.

(Note from Christine – Hearing Kimmy howling and yowling this morning was a very bad start to the day, as I thought for a moment she was in dreadful pain and hoped it wasn't some terrible premonition of what was to come. I found her hissing at Guinness, but he was on the other side of the glass – could she really be that scared of him? I decided that today was the day I would tell people what was happening with Kimmy. She was very popular in the village and everyone always asked after her and, for several days now, I had avoided being asked. Today when they asked, I would tell them – 'Kimmy has cancer,' I said in my head... trying to hear how it sounded, but then I amended it to 'Kimmy's living with cancer...' rather than 'Kimmy's dying of cancer.' This sounded so much better and more positive, and it made me feel better saying it. So I went out and, when anyone asked, I said Kimmy had cancer. Their faces filled with concern and I said 'She's living with cancer' and I kept saying it until it felt like the most natural thing to say. Kimmy would somehow live with this cancer – until she was ready to go.

I told Gaynor at Authors Online, my publisher, and she immediately sent me this kind story back. I did of course know it, but it is so lovely it never hurts to hear it again. It's a tear-jerker though.)

Rainbow Bridge

Just this side of heaven is a place called Rainbow Bridge.

When an animal dies that has been especially close to someone here, that pet goes to Rainbow Bridge. There are meadows and hills for all of our special friends so they can run and play together. There is plenty of food, water and sunshine, and our friends are warm and comfortable.

All the animals that had been ill and old are restored to health and vigour. Those who were hurt or maimed are made whole and strong again, just as we remember them in our dreams of days and times gone by. The animals are happy and content, except for one small thing; they each miss someone very special to them, who had to be left behind.

They all run and play together, but the day comes when one suddenly stops and looks into the distance. His bright eyes are intent. His eager body quivers. Suddenly he begins to run from the group, flying over the green grass, his legs carrying him faster and faster.

You have been spotted, and when you and your special friend finally meet, you cling together in joyous reunion, never to be parted again. The happy kisses rain upon your face; your hands again caress the beloved head, and you look once more into the trusting eyes of your pet, so long gone from your life but never absent from your heart.

Then you cross Rainbow Bridge together....

Author unknown...

Mum's been weird again today. I have no idea what she is up to but she is spoiling me rotten! I am making the very most of it.

8th September 2010

I want a nice, quiet day with Mum today, but every time we try to relax, the phone rings or someone drops by and I have to jump off the chair and hide under the bed. At one point, it is someone I don't know and I see her peering under the bed at me, her face all upside down. I wish they wouldn't do that. I hear Mum go out with her, but Mum comes back fairly soon and again I get the chance to jump back on the bed and lie beside her, purring. I do feel a bit strange. Sort of OK but just not myself and I only want to be with Mum, on our own, because I get scared when other people are around. I manage to force down two breakfasts, lunch and am about to have supper, when Noel from next door knocks on the door. Mum lets him in and I stand my ground in the living room. For once, I don't run from the room but just sit and look at him and then I cross towards his outstretched hand and let him stroke me because I like Noel. Mum looks amazed at this, as I do it for so few people, but I know Noel and I know he is a good person. His window sill is next door to ours and sometimes I sit on it and stare into his apartment. He seems to like that. They talk for a while and then they both bow their heads and, with their eyes closed, say some words and afterwards Mum seems happier than I've seen her for ages.

(*Note from Christine – Today was one of those days where, every time Kimmy was on the bed with me or sitting on my lap, someone would call by or the phone would ring. I knew they were all well-wishers, but I just wanted this precious time with Kimmy alone and we were both very tired. A friend called to show me her new car and my heart sank, as I really wasn't* able to summon up any interest in it although I made all the right noises. She talked about her brother's dog and how she had been put to sleep a few years ago without any notice and I listened numbly. I had gotten used to people telling me their own sad stories of pet loss, but hearing someone tell me of someone else's – not even their own – was not what I needed to hear although I do know she meant it well and kindly. I couldn't say no to a trip in her car, but I wasn't able to join in with her chat. If you read this – I do know you were trying to cheer me up and I am grateful for that, but it is just impossible to make someone feel better when they are losing a beloved pet and I was relieved to get home again and back to Kimmy.

An electricity salesman called next and was given short shrift and, when finally I pulled the curtains for the day, I just wanted to bring this trying day to an end. I was alarmed to first hear a heavy bang on the door and then see Noel, my neighbour, on my doorstep. I shouldn't have been dismayed because when he came in and settled into an armchair, he said only kind and sensitive things. Surprisingly Kimmy didn't run from him but went over to have her head stroked and my eyes widened with surprise.

'We're old friends,' said Noel and I laughed with surprise. Kimmy had friends outside of this flat?

'Yes, we chat all the time when I see her down the lane.'

'What lane?'

'The lane – down the hill…?'

I struggled to take this in. Was he telling me that my cat – my timid cat whom I knew so well – was wandering down the hill towards the busy road and stopping to chat to near strangers? That is exactly that he was telling me. Maybe she *was walking down to the woody bit where she had once gone missing for hours over a year ago. That was nice and safe and lovely for a cat – but that road – it was less so…! Did she have road sense that I hadn't credited her with?*

'She also sits on my window sill.'

I was learning new things about my cat.

I asked Noel, a retired Presbyterian Minister, if he would pray for Kimmy, but he said his faith would not allow him to pray for animals. He would pray for me, to give me strength in this sad and difficult time. Well, praying for me is the same thing as praying for Kimmy as we both want the same thing. I very gratefully accepted.

We bowed our heads as this kindly man said words that I hoped would bring me peace. And they did.

After he left I felt entirely different. I felt less sad, less depressed and possibly more able to cope for the first time in ages.

I felt like a new person.)

9th September 2010

I wake Mum up at five thirty as usual and she staggers out of bed to give me my breakfast, but I think she must have got it wrong. She gives me slightly yucky tuna – the stuff Jamie rejected – and I don't want it. I stomp back into her room to wake her again but can't – she's gone back to sleep. Later when she gets up and realises her terrible mistake, she immediately puts it right by opening Chicken Felix for me. Yum. I eat it hungrily and reward her with a purr and rub around her ankles. Sometimes us cats just like what we're used to.

I sleep most of the morning, napping in the middle of the bed, which she hasn't got round to making when I settle down for a good sleep. *Zzzzzzzzzzzzz.* I am sleeping quite deeply at the moment and, every time I wake up, I find Mum staring at me as if she has never seen me before. Why does she do that?

At lunchtime, I have a choice of dishes. I reject the salmon, as I just had it a few days before. Food just doesn't seem to taste the same these days. There was also some Felix, which I'd had for breakfast, but I manage a little more yucky tuna before going out of the window for a stroll.

Once in, I notice that Mum had changed all the sheets and I have a nice fresh bed. I do love clean bed linen. All us cats do. Usually I like to help her change the covers by lying on them as she straightens them out. That always makes her laugh. But I am getting a bit sick of her following me around so I opt to go *under* the bed for a while because she can't get at me there. Luckily I hear her go out and I am slightly relieved. A bit of peace and quiet. *Zzzzzzzzzzzzzzzz.*

In the evening, I pop out to explore the building site again, where I haven't been for a while. It's a warm evening and I love the feel of the sun on my fur, even though I can see Mum peering through the fence at me. I ignore her and get on with my business. Sometimes a cat has to just be a cat.

I come in *eventually* and am offered, salmon, tuna, Felix and some chopped up chicken, but I mew and mew until she offers me some Chicken Whiskas – delicious. I will probably go back to the other dishes later and finish them up too.

(Note from Christine – After chatting to my neighbour, Noel, and his offering up a prayer to make this all feel easier, I felt

slightly different about everything. Or maybe it was knowing and seeing that my timid little cat had a relationship with my neighbour that I had not known about. It may sound strange but when you see an animal one way and then you see them slightly differently you begin to understand that you don't know them as well as you thought. Kimmy had enjoyed an enormous amount of freedom at this new address and clearly was not quite as timid as I thought. If that were true then maybe she was a fighter? Other evidence was that she ate well – very well (although she was more fussy) – and was still asking to go out. She still played with her toys. She may well have been 'dying,' but she wasn't behaving like she was terminally ill and surely she would be by now? I owed it to her to find out what sort of treatment might be possible from Edinburgh. We had nothing really to lose at this point. I contacted Pete again and he told me of a great cat expert in Edinburgh – a professor – who was the top, top cat professional: Danielle Gunn-Moore, an oncologist. In other words, she was the only one who could save Kimmy. At least she might be able to offer alternative palliative care that might give her longer. I jumped at this and tried to contact Danielle Gunn-Moore by phone but learned that she doesn't speak to members of the public – she can be contacted by vet referral only. So I contacted Naomi at her surgery and her veterinary nurse, Kelly, emailed back to ask if I wanted Kimmy referred. Of course I did! OK so it may be that we would wait too long for an appointment and get it too late. It may also be that I wouldn't want to put Kimmy through a long journey if she had deteriorated, but for now it gave me hope to think that we may just – just – have an option now. I need to stress that Naomi had originally offered me this option, but I had declined it partly because I didn't realise Kimmy only had two weeks left, partly because I was too shocked by all the other news and partly because I had expected that it would be too much for a sick cat to go through this. I was still not sure it wouldn't be, but I was sure we should have the choice. Sometimes you just need a few days to get used to an idea and to help you look at things differently. OK so we were really clutching at straws now but sometimes straws are all we get. And we clutch at them gratefully and willingly.)

10th September 2010

I love the early part of the day when I feel really safe and loved – and have a full tummy. I am snuggled in beside Mum and she is stroking my little head. I feel good.

It gets noisier as the day goes on because the men are digging up the pavement outside our flat and everything is shaking as they do it. Mum keeps tutting and closing windows, but it really doesn't make much difference and I wonder why she doesn't join me under the bed – it's a lot quieter here.

It gets warmer and I am quite relieved to see her go out, as I like the peace and quiet while she is away and I can really sleep without her looking at me every few moments. I am not sure why she is doing this. I stay under the bed and, when I hear her return, I pad out, sleepily, to greet her. She doesn't disappoint and is soon spooning Whiskas into my dish. I eat with enthusiasm, having ignored the salmon and the tuna she has also put down for me in a little row. Us cats love a choice of what to eat but for some reason Mum doesn't normally do this for me.

The doorbell rings and I go to hide while Mum's friend Mercia comes in with her dog, Teddy (no relation to my former friend Teddy the cat from the last flat). Teddy is nervous and he also hides but in a different room to where I am hiding. I can hear their voices talking forever, but finally Mercia and Teddy go and I pad back into the room to show Mum I am OK. Then I go into the back bedroom and climb up onto the window sill and then up onto the open window where I sit for a while surveying all around me. It is a warm, glorious evening and I can smell grass and feel the sun on my face. I can also see the big black birds but what I can't see is Guinness, or Big G, as we also call him, who appears just as I jump down onto the patch of lawn to take an evening stroll. Where did he come from? I arch my back and hiss angrily whilst looking at the open window. Can I get in before him and before he bashes me? I hiss again and let out a long growl and, nimbly, I jump back onto the window and go inside. Mum comes running in shouting and the second I drop in, she slams the window shut, while Guinness hauls himself up onto his back legs all ready to come in after me! He is standing on his hind legs bashing at the window with his paws. Then she runs into our bedroom and closes the window there. I have already gone under the bed – not because I am scared you understand – no, I am just thinking a bit before I come out. Cats need time to think. I can hear Mum on the phone telling her friend Karyn about this latest attack. I like that Mum tells people every single thing I do. This is how it should be.

An hour later I saunter into the room where Mum is watching that big television of hers. I stare at her for as long as it takes for her to realise that I want some more food, and I am given a big plate. Then I clean my face and jump onto Mum's lap, where she starts to comb my fur (it's a bit knotted, as I haven't really been able to groom myself as well as usual). I yelp with pain and she is all upset and starts to stroke me and smooth my fur instead. I purr and then go over to the front window of the living room and jump onto the ledge where I can see out. Mum doesn't usually let me go out the front window, as she says it is safer around the back, but I don't understand that. If I go out the back window, I am round the front in just a few moments and tonight I think she sees that logic so she opens the window for me and I jump out onto the ledge. From here I can see all around me – although it is dark – but we can see in the dark and that is often when the night is most exciting. We smell the scent of everyone who has passed by that day and spot any little creatures that might be around.

(*Note from Christine – Every morning was like a fresh test for me. I needed to see that Kimmy was OK and that she was eating, and luckily she was alright on both counts. I concealed painkillers in her food and was glad to see she ate it hungrily, then I could go back to bed for another hour or so, content. I was sleeping longer and more deeply, possibly to make up for lack of sleep and possibly due to the change of season, but I struggled to get up at eight and normally found myself sleeping a bit longer, with Kimmy lying as close to me as she could get – purring. It was a magical time for me, as I could get close to my cat and spend every valuable moment with her, regretting all the time that we had ever spent apart.*

I felt positive enough today to go into Belfast to do some shopping and leave Kimmy for a while. I realised that she probably needed time to herself, just as I needed my own space, and it was a gorgeous day. I was still feeling lifted from the whole idea of someone in Edinburgh being able to help and that thought was energising. With Kimmy eating well I could be reasonably confident that we would at least get another whole day together. I didn't stay too long in town and was home a few hours later feeling very much better for the break.

I checked my phone and my email when I got home, but there were no messages about Kimmy and the weekend was approaching. I could feel that sense of relief that maybe we would get a little respite from good, bad or indifferent news. Maybe Monday (which surely was the day for news) would bring something resembling hope. There was nothing but a message that my favourite band, Horslips, were doing some gigs in November and December. I really hoped I would be able to attend them, but I knew by then that I probably would be available, and that made me feel slightly sad. It felt hard to be making plans for a future that may not include Kimmy.

Mercia and Teddy dropped by. He looked so much like Pip – Mercia's dog who had recently died, but he was different in many ways and he was timid. I didn't mind him being in the flat, as Kimmy was fine with dogs – especially shy dogs like Teddy – and she was under the bed anyway, Teddy under another one. Mercia said lots of kind things about Kimmy and, after a while, she got up to leave, to take Teddy out for a walk, as it was a beautiful evening – more like summer than autumn, with real warmth in the air and bright sunshine. But all knew that this was the dying part of the summer and soon the nights would be cold and dark – so it was important to make the most of it. I wanted this for Kimmy too and was glad when she went out of the window to the garden outside.

Just a moment later I was startled by the crashing sound of Kimmy making a swift return, hissing angrily. 'Big G' was on the window sill and was standing upright on his back legs trying to haul himself in the window to follow her in! I slammed the window shut and he hissed at me. Kimmy ran into the bedroom and I ran in after her to make sure the bedroom window was also closed. I was angry, as this was the time that Kimmy was safest in the garden and it was quite the nicest part of the day. Guinness had spoiled this for her and, as I needed to monitor her continued interest in going out, now I couldn't be sure if she stayed in because she was ill or because she was scared of Guinness. I really wished he would go away and leave us. I phoned Karyn to voice my frustration and because I knew she understood the whole Guinness-Kimmy interaction. Deep down, we both found it funny as well as annoying but right now – worrying. We spoke for a few minutes and discussed keeping a bucket of water by the window. I was not so sure. It was usually over so quickly that there was no time to throw water and it somehow felt a bit drastic as a solution. She told me about how Guinness had broken a neighbour's cat-flap by getting stuck in it. He had been sneaking in at night to steal food and had been well and truly caught! The thought of Guinness half in and half out of someone's front door really made me laugh.

I allowed Kimmy out of the front window later, as I felt that, from now on, I should deny her nothing she wanted to do and it was quiet outside and she appeared to have a good amount of road safety. Instead she sat on the window ledge for some time – just watching. Cats love to just sit and watch and I wondered if she was looking at all the things she loved and wondering how long she had to enjoy them for, and it made me feel incredibly sad again – although I realise that cats don't think that way. They live in the moment. I heard a thump and she was down on the path outside, wandering around the parked cars and the quiet area to the front of my apartment block. She looked OK and seemed to know what she was doing but I was still relieved when she came in about ten minutes later. She didn't stay in long however and mewed her disapproval when I tried to shut the windows again – so I let her out once more.

Then a second sense hit me and I picked up my phone. I didn't expect there to be a message, as I had already checked and I'd been in all evening so my heart sank when I heard the irregular dial tone letting me know I had a message. 'Let it be Mum… Let it be Mum,' I prayed as I hit the buttons that brought up the message. It was Naomi, the vet, sent at six thirty-eight and she was saying 'Edinburgh can't really do anything – the cancer is just too aggressive… I will try and phone you tomorrow.'

That was it; the final bit of hope was gone. And I had been on the phone when she called.)

Mum told me that Guinness got stuck in a cat flap. If I'd been there I'd have bitten his bottom and run off.

11th September 2010

(Note from Christine – I found a great organisation on Facebook called Animal Reiki Healing and I contacted them with photos of Kimmy and they agreed to send her Reiki healing as often as we liked. I took massive comfort from this and felt a great relief that someone else was looking after Kimmy now as well as me.)

Mum seems very busy on her computer so I amuse myself. I go in and out of the window and take some naps under the bed – away from everyone so I can get some peace and quiet. I try to clean around my face but can't get my tongue to work so I just Zzzzzzzzzzzzzzzzzzzzzzzz instead.

13th September 2010

I don't like my breakfast today – it has a funny taste and I feel slightly odd – just tired and not very well. I want to sleep it off – as us cats like to do – so I slide under the bed and settle down for a quiet day. But Mum gets all upset and keeps wanting me to come out and that makes me feel worse. Why doesn't she just leave me alone when I'm not feeling great?

(Note from Christine — I was upset when I saw Kimmy hadn't eaten her breakfast as she always did. She hadn't had her medication either – or just a bit of it – but I couldn't tell how much so wasn't able to risk giving her more. I felt my heart sink – especially as Kimmy's eyes looked distant and she appeared to be a bit floppy. She had never looked like this before so it had to be bad.

I called Mum and she came over and agreed with me that Kimmy looked distant and shared my worry about her not eating. I emailed Pete Wedderburn and he sent a very kind email telling me that perhaps this was 'The Time' and reminded me that we always knew it was coming – sooner rather than the later I had expected.

"Remember what I said – that the pain of losing her

cannot be avoided – whether it's this week, next week or if it had been in three or four years time. The pain is the inevitable other side of the coin of loving her so much. You can't have one side of the coin without the other. Focus on the wonderful time that you've had together, the positivity that she's brought into your life (and into so many other people's lives via your joint books). She was a lucky cat to find you (and vice versa). We all wish that we didn't have to lose those that we love, but it's a fact of life. We all lose friends, parents, brothers, sisters and pets. It hurts a lot but a life without that hurt would be a life without the pleasure and joy of the love that's been shared. We're lucky that most humans live for a long time, so we don't have to suffer loss so often – but with pets, we only get ten to fifteen years (usually). We can only make the best of those years, savouring them and being grateful for them... and try to cope as best we can with the loss. Life does continue afterwards, and there won't be another Kimmy, but there will be other loving creatures that'll creep into your life at some stage...

Do keep in touch – Pete

'No!' I wanted to scream. I wasn't ready! I just wasn't ready. I hadn't had her long enough and in no way was I prepared to have her put to sleep. But I did find great comfort and strength in Pete's words.

I knew Naomi had a surgery that evening at five so, if I was going to 'do it,' I would do it that night and not wait, but that would force me to make the decision to take her in rather than get a home visit. I didn't want to call the vet, as that was admitting defeat. I wanted to give Kimmy as long as possible to bounce back, if she was going to. That would mean I would 'know' by the evening and surely a short trip to the vet – to a vet I knew and liked – would be the quickest way. I couldn't decide, but I did tell Mum I would decide by four p.m. And we sat in silence, staring at each other while I tried to harden myself to doing the right thing for my cat. I allowed my head to rationalise the situation and tried to keep my heart out of it. I knew she had aggressive cancer and had been given a very short time to live. Pete was right – the time had just come earlier rather than later – and, as I knew she had to die, surely now was as good a time as any? I certainly didn't want to see her suffer.

By three p.m we were still in doubt as to whether Kimmy was really unwell or just being very quiet, so I said to Mum, 'If she wants to live, she has to give me a sign. She has to do something.'

I could see Kimmy in the hallway, heading towards the study and the open window. She wanted to go out! And out she jumped into the garden. That was sign enough for me! She wanted to go out – that wasn't what a dying cat would ask for. A few moments later she had returned and was asking for some food – I found some salmon in the fridge and she wolfed it down. Kimmy may well not have felt that great earlier but she was OK now. She had given me the sign I needed – so there would be no trip to vet or visit from the vet today!

As I hadn't eaten all day, I made myself something to eat but, as I ate it, it seemed to stick in my throat and I couldn't swallow. I had been so busy preparing myself for Kimmy's passing that I had almost reached that place where I could have gone through with it and then had gone to complete elation that she was OK again – the swing was too great and I was overcome with tearful emotion.

Later when I read my messages on Facebook, I discovered that Kimmy's Reiki healing had started that afternoon and I really liked to think that this had had something to do with her amazing 'recovery'. I told Pete about the Reiki healing by email, feeling sure he would be sceptical and he replied.

"My own dog Spot was seriously ill with liver failure a few months ago – He's thirteen and was badly jaundiced, not eating and extremely ill. I gave him full-on conventional treatment, but who doesn't look for other answers in such situations? My brother, a committed born-again Christian, prayed for him… Two days later, he turned the corner and has made a full recovery. So, I never say no. You just never know. Take whatever succour is available…"

Pete

Mum's really weird with me all day, checking up on me and doing that thing with her eyes where they get all wet. OK, so I didn't feel that great, but I feel better after a good sleep. When I come into the living room to see her and Gran I don't expect to get smothered in kisses. They really are a strange pair. I hope nothing is wrong.

14th September 2010

Mum and I have gone to bed and I sense that she is sad so I climb in with her and lie right on top of her hip as she lies sideways.

This is where I like to be – unless I lie on her chest which is also nice and sort of squashy. I am tired and want to sleep, but Mum is restless and won't turn out the light. It doesn't bother me but I know she won't sleep if it is on. A few times I wake and look at her. She says something about 'I'm very hot Kimmy. You're like an extra blanket,' but I notice she doesn't move me and, after a while, I think I'll try my luck. I hold her gaze and lick her hand and she knows what that means, although usually she says no. This time she says 'Kimmy, are you hungry?'

Am I? Of course I am hungry!

Mum is out of bed and I pad ahead of her to the kitchen and towards my dishes. Oh joy of joys, I am getting a very, very early breakfast. She puts down something delicious in a thick gravy and I tuck in hungrily. 'Now you're talking,' I think as I nom my way through the dish. It is a fairly small helping but enough to fortify me, so I run to the little room at the back of the flat and jump up onto the window ledge. I meow persistently until she gets the message. She seems to be saying yes to everything now. She opens the window. She doesn't normally let me go out after midnight. Two jumps and I am out – one up and then one down!

Oh the garden is lovely! The grass feels all thick and damp under my paws and everything smells so good – fresh and clean. There is a layer of sweet-smelling moisture over the lawn and the sky is alive with small stars. There are no builders, no nasty cars – nothing. Just me and the whole glorious darkness. I take a stroll to my favourite tree and stick my claws in before diving into the hedge and then down to the neighbour's and I stroll and stroll, watching and sniffing and taking care not to find Guinness, until after a long time, I come back in the way I left but with wet, dirty paws and a huge appetite.

Mum isn't asleep and greets me as if she's never seen me before. 'Kimmy!' she says, looking happier than she has done for ages. I meow urgently and angrily till she puts more food down for me and then we both go back to bed. I let her sleep for quite a while until I wake her for breakfast. But to be fair, she doesn't complain at all, although she looks a bit tired. She then stumbles back to bed for an hour and gets up only to offer me *another* breakfast, but this time I say 'no.' A cat has to think of her figure…

I spend most of the day dozing on the bed, feeling very content. There is no better way to keep a cat happy than to feed us well and let us doze on a warm bed or by a warm fire. And to reward her for treating me so well I allow Mum's friend, Mercia, to come in and stroke me, which seems to please Mercia a good deal. 'Kimmy …!' she keeps saying 'Yes, that's me!' I think. Maybe I should be this nice all the time, as it seems to result in more attention, which I don't always get when I hide under the bed.

Gran arrives to see me as Mercia is leaving. Everyone comes to see me these days and I feel very important. I stroll into the living room and let her play with me and my fishing rod toy. They seem to think I am a kitten again but it seems to make her and Mum very happy and I have to admit I am happy too. Whatever that food is that Mum got me is totally delicious!

(Note from Christine – Having not had a great day, I wanted to go to bed early and get it over with. But to my amazement, I couldn't sleep – I had so much going through my head and, with Kimmy lying on my side, I did feel very warm but was so

pathetically pleased to have her with me that nothing would have made me move her. So when she gave me a 'look' at one a.m, and licked my hand, I knew what she was saying. She was hungry – and so was I! I had barely eaten all day either, so I got up and followed her to the kitchen where I put down some IAMs chicken in gravy and was nearly tearful to see Kimmy eating it, while I ate a banana and some dried bread (my food stocks were very low!), Kimmy wanted to go out and although it was one a.m, I let her, as I felt that she should be allowed to do what she wanted and I knew I could stay awake until she came in. She returned just after two thirty looking thrilled with herself but hungry again and I couldn't have been happier to feed her. Knowing she would eat it, I was able to add her pain medication to the food and see that she ate every bit. What an appetite! Surely she couldn't be at death's door if she was eating so well and going out and enjoying herself? I felt the happiest I had felt for days and really didn't care that I was so tired. It had all been worth it. My cat was not going anywhere – just yet.

It occurred to me, as the day went on, that it was important not to let her see my stress or anxiety. I went out to get more IAMs, enjoying the time outside of the flat, safe in the knowledge that she was well at home. I had been very anxious the day before and I was sure Kimmy had picked up on it. Cats really can sense our fear, so I vowed to get out every day for a few hours and to give her a little space and not to fret too much – or not to show it. I also thought of the Reiki healing people (Animal Reiki Rescue) I had found on Facebook and all the prayers being offered for her and wondered if I was getting some spiritual help – especially when the Reiki people told me they had been sending out healing for me too. We all have a good deal to learn about life and I had learned a lot today.)

15th September 2010

After Mum has given me breakfast, we both go back to bed because Mum says it is still early. I cuddle up close and purr. I love these mornings we spend together, all warm and cosy in the big, warm bed. Mum stays in bed far later than usual but eventually gets up, saying she has to go to yoga or something. She hasn't been there for a while so I snooze on.

Later I have another delicious plate of something lovely and then, joy of joys, she turns on the fire for me so I can lie beside it – as close as possible – and toast my tummy. Just bliss. Most people know that, for cats, toasting our tummies is just the best thing of all!

Kimmy toasting her tummy

16th September 2010

(*Note from Christine – Waking up with a purring Kimmy this morning, I nearly did a double take. She was sitting just inches from me and I could see her face really clearly. It looked as if her fur, shaved for the biopsy, had grown back overnight and the bald bits were no longer glaringly obvious. Her stitches had dissolved and she tilted her head back as if to show me just a tiny dot under her chin – one last stitch. It seemed that she had healed herself overnight and, in my half asleep state, I allowed myself to dream that it was all OK now. She had somehow cured herself of the cancer and my prayers had been answered; the Reiki healing had worked. The feeling was so good that it lasted all day and I couldn't get over the fact that my cat was looking so well again – you could barely see any difference now from how she'd looked before. She had eaten her usual five a.m breakfast and had been out and here she was, eating again.*

I had to decide whether to take her to the vet, Naomi, again and this presented me with a problem – a problem of indecision. We were both feeling so good and was there any harm in wanting to stay that way a little longer? Naomi was hardly going to say 'Oh the tumour has gone' and, as we'd only had bad, bad and even worse news, I was scared we would hear more. I was also genuinely worried about putting her into her carrier and taking her back to see someone who had once hurt her so badly – albeit in order to help her. The one good thing about palliative care is that theoretically the animals shouldn't really have to go into the vet again and can be saved all that stress. And stress is not good for anyone – let anyone a little cat with cancer. But I wanted to see if Naomi agreed with me that Kimmy was looking well – maybe she could confirm that a miracle had happened and that the cancer had gone into remission. Or that the cancer was progressing slowly. Or maybe I wanted to stay in that bubble a little longer. Kimmy looked relaxed and happy, so I decided to go alone and discuss her with Naomi.

It is not uncommon for pet owners to see a vet alone under the circumstances, so no one was particularly surprised at the vet's surgery, but I think I saw a little anxiety on Naomi's face, as if she either thought I was bringing bad news or perhaps because she really had wanted to see Kimmy. We forget – or rather I had forgotten – that a vet-cat relationship is a concerned one too and, for a second, I regretted not bringing her.

I quickly and almost excitedly updated her on Kimmy's apparently good health and the quality of her life, her excellent appetite and zest for going out, the grown-back fur and the dissolved stitches. She nodded, smiling, and told me what to look out for.

'Check for swollen glands, bleeding, and a lolling tongue.'

Oh no. I hadn't thought of this.

'I wish I'd brought her in,' I said, meaning it, but Naomi understood and we discussed whether I could have a home visit when the 'time' came to put Kimmy to sleep and she agreed I could and said she would try hard to be there herself.

This, plus the fact that she said I had enough Metacam for two weeks and didn't need more, brought me back to earth with a bump. Didn't she think Kimmy would be here in two weeks?

We finished with a hug and both of us had tears in our eyes. I realised that, from Naomi's point of view, this was very upsetting too. It can't be easy, having a job where you frequently have to break very bad news to people. I left feeling just a little less upbeat than when I arrived.

By the time I got home I realised just how little time the vet's visit had actually taken. Kimmy would have only been out of the flat for half an hour at the most – just a mile up the road and a mile back. If I'd taken her, it would be over by now and we'd have both been home, and maybe I would have had some good news – would have known where I stood. I had an email from Pete.

"Glad you had a good meeting with Naomi. In general, I feel it's better to have as much info as possible about these things – no point in ignoring something that's going to cause a problem anyway, and if the news is good, it can be very uplifting. But remember, it won't change the course of the disease, so I don't know if I'd be suggesting that you take a chance with a no-appointment surgery. Might be better to wait a few more days and be sure that Kimmy doesn't have to wait, and that Naomi has plenty of time for you via the appointment. I wouldn't read anything into the few weeks of Metacam – that's just Naomi being practical – no point in taking more when you already have some. talk again soon
Pete"

So by trying to avoid hearing bad news, I had perhaps deprived myself of hearing good news. I took Pete's point and made an appointment for the following Thursday, when Naomi had her clinic, and just prayed we'd get another chance.

If you are not sure whether to bring a terminally ill pet to a vet's appointment, weigh up the options.

Is the surgery far away and how well does the pet travel? If it is a longish, stressful journey then perhaps you are justified in thinking twice about it. Do they mind going in their carrier or is it a mighty struggle to get them in the box? Would you want to know if the cancer was progressing faster or would you prefer just to take it a day at a time? And who are you thinking of – you or your cat?

And remember that your vet is there to help your pet not you – although they do obviously want to help both.

But if it really isn't an option, it can still be very useful to see the vet on your own, so long as you are honest about all the symptoms.)

Mum jumps out of bed saying that she is going to the vet's! The vet's – doesn't that involve me? No she is going on her own! I really am the luckiest cat in the world to have Mum – she even goes to the vet for me! I stay in bed, zzzzz.

17th September 2010

Mum is in a deep, deep sleep and is making those funny noises through her nose, but I am hungry. I jump on the bed and pat her face and lick her hand poking out of the duvet. With a start she wakes up, my tail inches from her face. Normally she bats me away and rolls over, with her back to me, but today (like most days this week), I don't have to ask again. She stumbles to the kitchen and, half asleep, begins to spoon my favourite food into a dish and then, still with her eyes closed, heads back to bed. A moment later and I am back, pushing back the curtains with my nose and mewing. Again she stumbles to the window and throws it open. Miraculous! She really doesn't like me going out like this, so I do a runner before she can change her mind. This time I do a tour of the building site to see how the funny houses with no windows (though now they have

roofs) are looking, then I go into each neighbour's garden in turn to sniff around before heading off back home for another breakfast – served by a still sleepy Mum.

She doesn't look great when she wakes up. She says something like, 'If I didn't have tickets to book online at nine a.m, I'd go back to bed,' but instead she settles herself down at her computer, yawning. The phone rings and I hear her speak – or rather listen for ages and then say, 'OK… well, it doesn't take long to go to the vet's, so pick me up on the way. No wait – I'll come round.'

The vet's? Well it doesn't take *me* long to hide under the bed while Mum frantically finds clothes to pull on. She doesn't even bother looking for me – a few minutes later I hear the door banging and she is off. Is she going without me again? Is this now the norm? That she will go to the vet every time I have to?

She comes back later and it turns out that this time it was Jamie, Gran's cat, who wasn't well and I feel very sorry for him. Maybe they will cut his chin open and then stitch him up and send him home bleeding? Poor Jamie.

I stay well under the bed for as long as possible, coming out only for a little lunch and to see if she's put the fire on. She hasn't, so I go back to bed. Later on, I make a big fuss of Mum because she looks tired and sad today, but I am dribbling a bit and Mum doesn't seem to mind me dribbling on the carpet. Funny that – she doesn't seem to mind anything I do these days. She must really love me.

Just when we settle down for a whole evening of TV watching (hopefully with the fire on), she suddenly jumps up from her arm chair and goes out, and drives off leaving me all alone. I think I spoke too soon when I said she must really love me! I sulk by the 'off' fire for a while and then go back to bed, only to wait in the hall when I hear her key in the lock *ages* later. Greetings over, I do a late night inspection of the flat to see that all is in order, while Mum gets herself ready for bed and, guess what, in Mum's bathroom, something very important is missing – my litter tray! Ok, so I still have one in the other bathroom – and I hardly use that, as I prefer to do my business outside – but the very least I expect is TWO trays. What if I get caught short and don't feel like going to the other bathroom? Or what if she is in there? Or what if my other tray isn't perfectly clean? I give her a look to curdle milk and shame her into going outside and retrieving my other tray from the bin store and filling it with litter. That's more like it. Us cats like order.

(Note from Christine – Kimmy woke me around four and I fed her and let her out the bedroom window. When she came in, I gave her more food and her medication. I always thought that letting her out when it was quiet like this, and allowing her to run around, gave her an appetite to ensure she ate the food with the pain relief in. And also I couldn't really deny her anything that she wanted at the time, but I was exceptionally tired when I finally got up at around eight thirty. I was tempted to just go back to bed, but I wanted to book some concert tickets for Horslips online when they went on sale at nine and I had

promised myself a trip to the gym to my Spin class. I hadn't been for ages – the yoga class had been cancelled a few days before – and I was keen to get some exercise and see my friends. I had also decided to give Kimmy some peace in the mornings and it was an opportunity for me to have a bit of a break. I would have some coffee after the class and would be back by late morning and that felt blissful to me, even in my exhausted, baffled state. What I didn't expect was a call from my mother just before nine, in a panic about Jamie. 'He's not himself,' she cried down the phone. 'I am so worried.' The timing may have been terrible, but I could hardly refuse to go with her when she had been so supportive with Kimmy, so scrubbing my plans, I rushed into the bedroom to throw on whatever I could find, then went round to her house to help her get Jamie.

Unfortunately, Jamie must have had a sixth sense or he possibly even heard the word 'vet' and did a runner. So we had to cancel the appointment and remake it for after lunch, and I went home and missed my class, but caught up on a bit of writing.

Mum arrived later, Jamie now found and in his carrier. He was duly taken to the vet – possibly the last place on earth I wanted to be – and given a totally clean bill of health. 'He's fine,' said the vet in reply to Mum's theory that he was not 'himself' despite having no real symptoms. 'He's just a bit fat.' Oh, how I laughed at this. Jamie might have to go to Fat Club!

She was charged twenty-one pounds fifty for the privilege of knowing her precious cat was okay and I must admit to feeling jealous. I'd have paid far, far more than that to hear Kimmy was OK. I suppose all the stress over Kimmy had made Mum more anxious about Jamie and more watchful for anything –

anything I had missed with Kimmy. It had affected her badly too.

With the day all fragmented now, there was little chance of me getting out so I just spent some quality time with Kimmy instead. It occurred to me that Kimmy had now had the two weeks originally predicted for her and was still doing well. I prayed that she would have more time.)

18th September 2010
(Note from Christine – Messages were flooding in for Kimmy on Facebook and Ann Scarborough sent me a lovely saying, which her vet had given her, by Sir Walter Scott, no less. It is about dogs but applies just as well for cats.

"I have sometimes thought of the final cause of dogs having such short lives and I am quite satisfied it is in compassion to the human race; for if we suffer so much in losing a dog after an acquaintance of ten or twelve years, what would it be if they were to live double that time?"
Sir Walter Scott

19th September 2010
Mum seems happier these days and she allows me to do anything I want. Just to test my theory I wake her at three a.m for breakfast and then again at seven and she doesn't complain – she just staggers about, putting food out on a plate for me and then she goes back to bed and, a few moments later, I jump in beside her. Then she gets up and eats her own breakfast and

goes out on her bike. From the window sill, I watch her go and think to myself 'a nap or a good wash?' As washing is quite difficult for me right now, I decide on a nap.

She comes back with some different food for me, but I don't like it. I wish she would realise that us cats like to eat what we're used to, not this horrible fancy stuff – tinned fish and something exotic sounding. I watch while she puts down dish after dish before I turn up my nose at all of them, and so she opens the packet of IAMS for me – that was all I wanted in the first place. I am interrupted by Gran's arrival and she has bought me a gift! She's brought a packet of tissue paper! I love to sit on tissue paper, but the piece I have is getting a bit crumpled, so now I have lots of nice fresh pieces and Mum puts some in each room, so wherever I am, I can sit on that lovely paper, which makes a delicious crinkly sound and feels smooth and cool underneath my bottie.

Then she puts the gas fire on for me and, after toasting my tum, I ask to go out of the front window (normally she says 'back window Kimmy', but tonight she opens it) and I jump onto the ledge and just sit and watch the world outside. I feel safe like this. Half in and half out. Most of all I love smelling the night air and looking out for any intruders that might come by. This, for a cat, is bliss and not that different from how Mum spends her evenings staring at a box with people and strange sounds. The houses over the road now have roofs and some have glass in the windows too, but they still don't look like proper houses yet. A high-pitched noise is coming from one of the cars parked in front of our house and a little light is flashing. Cats don't need televisions; we can see interesting things just by looking out a window.

(Note from Christine – I cycled to Carrickfergus, a small town four or five miles away, as it was such a glorious day. I was trying to get out for a few hours every morning to give us both a bit more normality. I realised that I had found some peace and contentment these past few days despite the terrible anxiety I'd felt before. For possibly the first time in my life I was 'living in the moment,' something that few of us normally do. I was trying to forget the events of the past weeks and just concentrate of having Kimmy today – making each day special and not thinking of the future or planning ahead in any way. We were OK today and had been yesterday. Tomorrow could take care of itself. This is the way cats live. Kimmy probably didn't know she was ill and certainly didn't know how serious it was, so she wasn't wasting away her days worrying. I had to do the same. By living in the moment, I was enjoying my life a good deal more and felt more 'protected'. If we try not to worry, life in turn becomes less worrying. I hoped I could hold on to this new found wisdom for as long as possible – but there I was thinking of the future again. I needed to just take a day at a time.)

20th September 2010

I don't feel quite so good today. I can't get rid of that funny taste in my mouth and it feels sort of strange. I've asked for food often, just to try to get rid of the taste, but my tongue feels odd in my mouth – as if it is a bit too big. I was embarrassed when Mum caught me dribbling earlier. A great long bit of drool hung from my mouth, nearly touching the floor. Mum wiped it away with a tissue but another bit appeared just after.

(Note from Christine – I was worried about Kimmy by bedtime. She had eaten well but was quieter and her eyes looked a bit sleepy all day. She seemed a little ... sad in some way, as if something was not right. I prayed that it was my imagination.

I decided to set Kimmy's auto feeder box up again – on a timer set to three a.m, so she could eat during the night – as I knew she liked to do – without waking me. It had been out of action for a while, as Kimmy had broken it by trying to open it ahead of the alarm, but I had managed to get it to work again. This might give me a bit more sleep...)

21st September 2010

Mum's fussing over me today, although she goes out and leaves me to nap for a while in the morning. She goes to her yoga class again. That always makes me laugh because cats are naturally good at yoga. We are always doing downward, er, cat stretches. She used to do it on a mat at home and I would sit on the mat while she did it or sometimes I would jump on top of her. I would sit on the back of the mat, catching her legs when they shot out behind her, and then I would go to the front of the mat when she put her hands down. In fact, when Mum does yoga, I am *everywhere* on her mat. You know the rhyme – 'the cat sat on the mat'? Well that is me. But for now, I please myself by putting my back leg behind my ear and biting my toes. I am fairly sure she couldn't do that.

Later on Mum gives me some excellent food – fish that she has cooked in the oven and allowed to cool, followed by special chicken slices. Oh, the bliss of all this – and she plays with me and my fishing rod toy, so I really get a workout. I, of course, work up an appetite for another snack – and guess what? She lets me have one! I think she must have noticed I am feeling a bit off colour because she can't do enough for me today and, come to think of it, she's been spoiling me for a while now. About time too! She's even set up my pop up feeder – so life can't get any better!

Then she puts on the TV in the smaller back-room and lies on the couch. I think she is feeling very tired from her yoga, but I like it when we are in this room because the back garden is just outside the window, which she opens for me, and I can go in and out and feel protected from 'anyone' – and by 'anyone,' I mean Guinness. I jump out and then come in again and repeat this a few times until I am inside again but sitting on the desk, looking out. I can see that small person, Michael, with his mum, walking around our garden and I narrow my eyes. Then I hear the small person's mum say, 'Look, Michael, it's Kimmy!'

'Kibby!' yells the small person and then, I am ashamed to say, I am cross and hiss at the little boy before jumping down, and I run off, leaving Mum to say 'sorry' for me.

23rd September 2010

Mum is acting strangely. She has gotten up early to feed me, (although not quite as early as usual, thanks to my pop up box) but after she's had her own breakfast she keeps looking over at me and I notice that she has closed the bedroom door, so I can't go in there. She never does things like that – unless – unless she is up to something and that usually means – the vet!

I do a good job of pretending I haven't noticed she is acting odd and mew for extra chicken, which miraculously I get, and then I mew piteously for the bedroom door to be opened. She never says no to me. Once inside, I am under the bed where I know she can't get me.

'Kimmy!' she yells.

She leaves me there long enough for me to relax and start to snooze, but then I see her upside down head, looking at me. 'Kimmy…' she says, calling me out. Well not flippin' likely. I know what is happening now and I don't like that vet anymore!

'I'm coming in,' says Mum, lying flat on her tummy and shuffling herself under the bed, which is full of old cases and her spare duvet, so it is hard to navigate. I hear her buttons popping too, on the shirt she's wearing as she drags herself along the ground. I merely get up and change position so I am even further away. She can't reach me!

I feel the bed being pulled away and suddenly there is ceiling above me but nothing else! I run under the spot where the bed was, but she moves it again. Oh this is mean… moving a cat from her hiding place is just not on!

I run from the bedroom to the window, which I hope will be open. If it is, I will do a runner – but it is closed and I feel Mum's strong hands grab me, and a second later I am in that dreadful carrier again. This is so not fair. Meow!

I am sure you know what happens next? Yes, Gran appears in her little car and I am loaded into it and a few minutes later we are at the vet's, waiting in that small room, and I am staring at a very miserable-looking dog with a long, droopy face, a fat Labrador and 'something' in a cardboard box. They look about as happy as I feel. After what seems like forever – and the droopy dog has come out looking angry – Naomi comes out and calls out my name. 'Kimmy!' she says, coming towards us.

I am carried into her room but resist coming out of the carrier for as long as possible. I hold onto the sides of the box and hiss loudly, taking several moments to drop out. I am about to lash out at Naomi, but Mum smoothes my fur and firm hands grip me. I hear them talking and actually laughing a bit and then my mouth is forced – yes, forced open – and Naomi takes a look. Whatever she says makes Mum look so happy that she cries a bit and they both look very pleased. I run back into my carrier, but not before Mum flips me over to show my tummy to the vet and they both have a good giggle at it. Flippin' cheek…!

Then I am home and, as a punishment, I make Mum give me three more slices of that delicious chicken before I am satisfied and I settle down to meditate on my piece of tissue paper. On my back with my paws in the air and tummy up. Total bliss… I can't stay angry with Mum for long.

(Note from Christine – I slept badly and woke with a sense of dread. I hated taking Kimmy to the vet and dreaded what we might hear. It seemed a shame to risk taking away my last remaining inkling of hope, but I felt I owed it to Kimmy to find out what was going on. If the news was good then that could be celebrated and if it was bad, perhaps we would have to make plans, but what scared me most was that Naomi might want to put her to sleep there and then and I didn't want that – or rather I didn't want Kimmy to be so ill that it had to happen. Chasing her round my bedroom and then catching her made me nearly chicken out, but I held steadfast and decided I would face whatever was coming. I was actually glad it was a dark, wet day until I realised that this might be some sort of bad omen. Surely nothing good could come out of a day like this?

By the time we had got to the vet's, I was already wishing we'd stayed at home, but luckily there was only one grumpy looking dog ahead of us and a few other animals that had come later. Having checked in, I felt leaving would be too over-dramatic and I didn't think Kimmy looked especially unhappy, but before I could get too worried, Naomi came out and called us into her surgery.

She was terribly gentle and kind to us both. She didn't haul Kimmy out of her carrier but talked to me while Kimmy made her mind up to join us, albeit reluctantly. She was pleased that Kimmy was doing normal things and taking her medication and we joked about her very healthy appetite, but finally there was nothing left to say and Kimmy had to be examined. I took a deep breath as Naomi opened her mouth (removing the final stitch) and felt around her chin.

'This hasn't changed at all since I first saw it,' she said, clearly delighted and I loudly thanked God and brushed away a tear. 'It hasn't grown at all,' she said, full of wonder. 'She really is an amazing cat. She's doing well.'

Never had news been taken with such relief and happiness. OK so she still had cancer but it was not progressing – yet. We still had some time together and I was sure it was the prayers and Animal Reiki Healing as well as a lot of love and care from me and her friends. We would still have to face the inevitable, but we could put if off for weeks or hopefully months yet. She gave me another month's supply of Metacam, her pain relief, and it comforted me to think that maybe we might need another one after that...

I treated the waiting room to the biggest smile I had given anyone that year and I didn't stop smiling for the rest of the day as I shared the news on Facebook and by email and phone. But to put it in perspective – Kimmy did still have cancer – it was just growing slower than everyone first thought. I wanted a miracle but this would do for me. I felt so good about it that I booked myself a day trip to London – life had to go on.)

24th September 2010

Mum gets all excited because she is going out shopping. I have the place to myself while she is away and I doze in peace. Most days now, if she isn't swooping down on me to smother me in kisses, she is waving one of my fishing rod toys above my head or taking a photograph. Sometimes cats just like to be admired from a distance and I do feel tired these days. When she comes back, she is loaded down with bags and looks a bit guilty.

I think it is probably just as well that cats don't have credit cards.

But she tells me Donna at my solicitor's office (Caroline is my solicitor, if you've read my last book) has bought a copy of my Irish Diaries and has given an extra five pounds donation. Isn't that kind!?

25th September 2010

I spend the day going in and out of the window from the flat to the garden outside and, just to be extra brave, I go through the little gap in the hedge into the school next door to us. It is nice and quiet, as the kids aren't there today. I also run into the building site at the side of our building. I like that, as again it is peaceful so I can really nose around. When I hear Mum call I run… and run towards her and she seems very pleased to see me. 'Kimmy, you run like a racehorse!' she says. 'Well, whatever. Isn't being a cat enough?'

Then I spend the evening sitting on a paper bag. This is my sort of a day.

(Note from Christine – I noticed for the first time, properly today, how uneven Kimmy's face was. She was lopsided and the dribble coming from her mouth was near continuous. It must have annoyed her a great deal. Her grooming was not quite as good as it had been either – she was struggling to manage. But in herself, she seemed as healthy and full of life as ever. Watching her run to me from the building site like a horse, it was as if nothing was wrong.)

29th September 2010

I am starting to worry a bit about Mum. She seems to be very tired and has a sniffle. She says she is getting a cold, but I hope that is all it is. I really hope she isn't seriously ill. I try to cheer her up by eating all my food and asking for more… and more. I like eating. Later on, a man comes with our grocery delivery from the big supermarket. As he brings the stuff in – including food for me – he sees me (before I can hide) and says 'That's one fat cat!'

Mum is furious and slams the door after he's gone. I am glad she is finally getting to realise that I don't like being called fat!

I go to my litter tray and furiously dig in it, throwing cat litter all over the place. Fat indeed!

102

30th September 2010

Mum's gone out for lunch and left me. I am feeling a bit tired today so I sleep by the radiator in the bedroom that we share. Gran looks in on me at some point but I am too sleepy to say much to her and she seems worried. Sometimes I just don't feel that well – I don't know why but I wish they wouldn't fuss. I will probably feel OK when I've had more sleep. Much later, when Mum gets back and we're both asleep, I wake Mum because I realise I am now hungry. She gives me a dish of something but I don't fancy it anymore.

3rd October 2010

I watch Mum as she sleeps and decide to let her see my chin and my face, as they are bothering me a bit lately. I am a pretty girl with a big appetite, but I have realised that 'something' is wrong. I know Mum knows it too. So I lie close to her and press my head towards her. She wakes, and sleepily she looks at me closely and then she strokes my fur, very gently.

'I know, Kimmy … I know.'

4th October 2010

I couldn't get Mum to wake up and had to walk all over her purring until she said sleepily, 'Go away Kimmy!' Now, this is something she hasn't said for ages and I am a bit surprised. What has happened to the new treatment I've been having? I then have to resort to smacking her face with my paw until she stumbles out of bed, stopping to use her litter tray and then scraping food into my dish, opening a window, and all without so much as prising her eyes open. Yes, she can now do these things in her sleep. And sleep she does because, after I have eaten my delicious breakfast, I jump back into bed. Later I decide to go out for a bit. I am feeling good today and decide to spend the day awake and in the lovely sunshine, and there is Mum sleeping!

(Note from Christine – Kimmy woke me at five a.m and I was so tired that I tried to roll over, but eventually she got the better of me and I did manage to give her breakfast and put her medication in without opening my eyes – so I could get back to sleep as quickly as possible. Unfortunately I then overslept, but it was a beautiful day again with bright sunshine and blue skies, so I had a walk along the beach to the pet shop to get her some more food – she seemed to like a big selection and, as I walked, admiring the day, I prayed again to let Kimmy live and give me a miracle. 'Please God, you have given us this glorious day – please give me another miracle and let Kimmy live. Not forever, of course I understand, but let her not die now – not like this. I felt comforted afterwards and energised.

When I got back, Kimmy seemed super charged as well. She went out several times and, when inside, she sat looking out of the window or eating, and she looked so much better too. She was dribbling less and seemed very alert. Was it so strange to think that she was getting better? And with hindsight I wondered if I might have been better not asking how long she had. It doesn't really help to 'know' and it can just add to the stress. I felt a lot better when we got past the two weeks she had originally been given. Vets really can't know for sure how long – so why do we ask? If you get a cancer diagnosis – just assume your pet is on borrowed time for days, weeks, months or possibly a year. Unless we are planning a house move or a holiday – do we really need to know?

You have two choices with cancer – you can see it is as something that is killing you and that you'll die of, or you can learn to live with it – just take each day as it comes. I was trying hard to learn to live with Kimmy's cancer. We were living with it – not waiting to die. And the difference in attitude is amazing. Maybe we'd cracked it? Maybe positive mental energy and a lot of love had made this all 'go away'?)

6th October 2010

I've learned that I get more food if I turn my nose up at everything she gives me. She is always keen to please these days and I don't like a lot of what she gives me. It's OK, but nothing tastes quite right these days. She gives me chicken Whiskas, which I haven't had for ages and I like it. It has some taste.

(Note from Christine – Kimmy was getting harder to please with her food and of course I wanted to give her something she liked, and she needed to have her Metacam. She was in and out of the window a lot today, but looking at her, I had a shock when I realised that the tumour was now more noticeable. Her face looked a bit more lopsided and swollen. Was it me or had it gotten bigger?)

7th October 2010

Mum took me to the vet place again to see Naomi and she looked at my face and made a big fuss of me. I really like Naomi even though she is a vet. She is always nice to me and doesn't hurt me. 'I don't think it has grown much,' she tells Mum who looks very pleased indeed. But you'd think they would just leave it at that – no! I get put on those stupid scales again and am told I am five point three kilos. Mum smiles weakly but for the first time ever she doesn't seem pleased that I have lost a little weight.

8th October 2010

Mum says she has a cold and isn't feeling that well. I am worried about her because I know that sometimes she doesn't look happy but when we are both together like this it feels just perfect, as if no harm can come to either of us.

11th October *2010*

(Note from Christine – Kimmy was refusing most of the food I put down for her and this was making me frantic, as we were judging how well she was by how much she was eating, and she needed to take her Metacam. She did seem hungry though – it must have been something to do with the discomfort in her jaw rather than her appetite. I gave her several different things and on about the fifth option she finally ate. I felt overwhelming relief. She had never been a fussy cat before – far from it.)

13th October 2010

Mum gets up early this morning and says she is going to London for the day. She gives me my breakfast and tells me to be 'good' for Karyn and Fred who are looking after me. Now, you might recall from my earlier diaries that, when Mum went to London before (when we lived in Bath), she would come back all 'sooty' and smelling a bit strange. I can only imagine that London is a very dirty place.

I spend the day waiting for her to get back. I hear the door open a few times and I come out to see who it is. I try not to look upset when I see it isn't her; I can't help it. Karyn and Fred are very kind to me and, at one point, Karyn lies under the bed, where I am hiding, passing treats to me. I can smell her cats on her – I met them when I lived at the other place. I think they are called Flossie, Fudge, Skippy and Truffles... yes, that's it. I eat the treats and try to look as pathetic as possible.

Mum comes back a bit flustered. 'You know Kimmy, I could get a taxi and a plane and a tube train and a bus to London and the friend I was meeting for lunch who lived in London couldn't even get on the right train to Richmond, so she ended up miles away...' Mum has spent much of the day waiting for her friend to arrive and had to leave soon after she finally got there. I think that is quite funny, but Mum doesn't seem too happy, although she says she is pleased to be home. 'I am not going away again,' she says, rubbing my tummy and topping up my bowl. 'It was fun, but I missed you all day.' I pretend I am starving and get an extra big portion before jumping out of the window.

16th October 2010

I feel very hungry today and am pleased when Mum obliges me by putting down a never-ending range of full bowls of delicious food. She has started to heat the plates as well, by running them under a warm tap. That is such a good idea, as we cats like our food at blood temperature! Afterwards she grooms me with a brush, as I don't seem to be managing that so well these days. My fur is a bit matted and it hurts a bit, as she has to tug the brush through. I try not to bite her.

19th October 2010

Mum goes shopping again and comes back with lots of new things. I am pleased because I get to lie on the paper Primark bag all evening – it's just the right Kimmy-size. She did lots of shopping there. Total bliss.

20th October 2010

Mum had to take back some of the Primark things, so I have to give her the bag back. That is annoying, but I wonder what the shop say when they see bits of my Kimmy-fur and drool on the outside of the bag?

(Note from Christine – Someone said on Facebook that maybe Kimmy would have 'years' now and told me about another cat who had lived on after a cancer diagnosis. I felt quite upset, although I knew they were trying to make me feel better. I really didn't want false hope and was trying not to think 'how long,' but I did know that Kimmy wouldn't have years – this was a very aggressive cancer. I wish people didn't always feel the need to say things that aren't true just because the truth is too scary to say. But on the plus side, Kimmy had a lot of fans and

they all cared about her very much. I was taking great comfort from their messages of support and by writing about our day to day lives and how we were dealing with this.)

21ˢᵗ October 2010

(Note from Christine – Jason, the foreman here on the building site, told me about something he had read about how diet can make a real difference with cancer – especially supplements – and I emailed Pete Wedderburn to see what he thought. He suggested a DHA Omega Three oil capsule, which had had some positive feedback, and I sent off for some immediately. It couldn't do any harm and might do some good. I took Kimmy to see Naomi again and once again she didn't think the tumour had grown, although we both noted that Kimmy wasn't grooming so well – her fur looked dirty and matted – and I needed to do her grooming for her. But despite this, it felt like a good day.)

30ᵗʰ October 2010

I love this time of year although it is not warm anymore and there is the noise of fireworks outside that I remember from when we lived in Bath – they had them there too. I am enjoying going in and out of the window, although in the evening, Mum closes all the windows and tells me I am not going out. I then decide to sleep, first on my ladybird cushion, which I've not been on for a while, and then on the ironing board – it is still nice and warm from when Mum used it earlier. There are always plenty of places for a cat to sleep – especially me, but I do admit that my mouth is feeling quite sore, as if someone has punched me, and I am feeling quite tired – more tired than usual.

31st October 2010

Mum isn't letting me out and I don't know why, as I love fireworks and I enjoy sitting on the window sill looking out at them. Everything has changed so much since I lived in the pink house in Bath. There, we had lots of cars and noise and I just had a walled courtyard, but now I can go outside whenever I like and I can see lots of clear sky and birds and trees. And tonight I can see lots of lights filling the sky and flashing across them with loud bang-ey noises. It feels good and my life feels perfect.

1st November 2010

(Note from Christine – I had a bit of a clear out today and found lots of old photos of pets – pets we had as kids that were no longer with us – and memories came flooding back. That was a bitter sweet moment that made me feel happy and sad. I looked at Kimmy and noticed that she looked very dirty especially around her face. She just wasn't able to groom at all now and looked a bit neglected. It wasn't like her, as she had always been so perfectly groomed. It forced me to realise that 'soon' I might have to make The Decision and I really didn't want to. Wouldn't it be so much easier if Kimmy just passed away in her sleep? I knew that wouldn't happen, but for now the quality of her life was still good. She was getting DHA oil in her food, and so was I, although I hoped for Kimmy it wasn't too late.

I would try and find some sort of cat shampoo and give her a good brushing. Maybe buy some scissors and try to cut out the tangled bits of matted fur.)

Winter

3rd November 2010

I feel pretty tired today and just sleep. I dream that I am chasing a big field of rabbits and eating them all up. When us cats aren't feeling well, we sleep because it is very healing. In the evening, I climb out of the window and go for a stroll around the building site. I like it when the builders have gone home so I can see what they have been up to. Winter now seems to have arrived. The dark nights come earlier and it's wet outside, but I am enjoying the feel of the wind and rain on my fur. It makes me feel alive. By the time I get home, Mum screams, 'Kimmy, you are soaking!' and dries me with a towel, and moans that I look as if I have been swimming in a puddle. Well, in a way, I have.

5th November 2010

Mum gives me cream and fish oil. What a delicious combination. What more can I say?

(*Note from Christine – I had been in touch with Ginger, a pet psychic from Indiana in America that I had met via the Facebook*

Pets Reiki page. She had emailed a few times because she had been helping me come to terms with Kimmy's illness and she messaged me to say that she had 'been in touch' with Kimmy (I assume by looking closely at a photograph of her? I really don't know how she does it). Kimmy had 'told her' that she wanted cream and that she was OK to take the supplements that I had got her. She also said Kimmy 'didn't want' the jaw operation that I had already ruled out – she thought it would 'be stupid.' Ginger said that Kimmy knew that she was ill but wasn't in pain, although she did feel discomfort. Most poignant of all, Kimmy had told the wonderful Ginger that she had noticed how I treated her differently these days. I was more fussy and attentive and she found this puzzling. She also told Ginger that she knew I loved her. So that felt very touching and made me cry a little. I went out and bought her cream and put the fish oil supplements in it and, of course, Kimmy lapped it up.

How does Ginger work and know these things? How does she communicate? I have no idea. But I do not for one second doubt her gift. Oh, and she doesn't charge for this so there is nothing to be gained for her – she really does have a genuine gift. These kindnesses from strangers were just enormously heart-warming and made this all so much easier to bear and made this time so precious

This is what Ginger wrote:

"I made a connection with Kimmy! Please know I don't diagnose or treat & only work on "feelings" Please ask vet about everything first.

I asked her why she didn't like her meds. I got the word fish oil. I got "I want cream." I asked if she would

take supplements for her immune system. She said yes. I asked if she was in pain. She said "It's just annoying" She thinks her illness makes you do funny things & she doesn't understand.

I asked her about toys. She said she had a few she didn't always play with but they were hers. I see them as blue/purple. I asked if she went outside. She likes to go out for cool air but it's getting too chilly & she comes in to take a bath & nap. She came across with a lot of joy and happiness and feels you love her. I asked if she should get an operation. She said "That would be stupid!

Peace & blessings Ginger"

After reading that, I really felt I had to be a lot more normal for Kimmy!)

6th November 2010

Mum has been sitting at her laptop and she is laughing a lot. 'Hey Kimmy, remember when we used to write Clawless with you as Clawdette!' Well no, I have no idea, as this is some silliness she got up to, but she is laughing and looks happy and I like that.

(Note from Christine – A few years earlier, on United Cats, I had channelled Kimmy's rather pampered and aristocratic personality to devise a soap opera for cats (we called it a soap opurra). Kimmy was to play her alter ego, Clawdette, working in the world of fashion. A growing number of cats joined in to play the other characters. At best it was hilariously funny, as

the plots got more and more outrageous and, at times, it was annoying, as 'artistic squabbles' would break out from time to time when someone took a plot in the wrong direction or made some other mistake. For the best part, our writers (Ann Scarborough, Etta Finta, Cathrine Garnell, Myra Strydom, Rebecca Gresham, Anne Sutton and Rachael Sharma) had the most enormous amount of fun. Writing from all over the world, in different time zones, it was often the first thing I checked when I woke up in the morning and the last thing I looked at before bed. It had all pretty much fizzled out about a year ago when, one by one, each writer had found they had less time to write and we had fewer ideas, but now on Facebook, Mara, Jan and Etta were reminding me of the ridiculous plots we had invented.

'Remember when Clawdette got kidnapped and it turned out she was just upstairs in the attic?' said one.

'And when she had the artistic hissy fit and walked off the set in a rage because someone suggested she wore support pants?'

'And the Catties!' They had been like the BAFTAS or Golden Globes but for our cats. Kimmy had won several awards for her portrayal of Clawdette and a huge number of laughs as well.

It got me thinking and I went looking for the PDF files we had made up of each 'series' – could I make our stream of consciousness, written by at least six (often more) writers, sound coherent as one piece of work? Well, I'd give it a go. It was funny; it made me laugh and right now I had the time. If I got it into any sort of shape I would approach the other writers and ask them what we should do with it. I felt delighted to have found a creative way to cheer myself up and I set to work at once by reading what we'd written.

(extract from Clawless)

" ... Clawdette paced up and down the library of Solange's pent-house apartment, her nose twitching with envy. How she would love to have this contemporary sunny place instead of the old mansion she lived in. It was hundreds of years old and filled with things called 'hair-looms' that she liked to scratch. Why didn't the boys ever like to have anything new? Hadn't they heard of IKEA? She stood out of the sun for a moment, fearing that it would fade her fur.

Damnit where was that cat? And why was she being kept waiting?

She looked around the room and noted that, although it was a library, it contained almost no books at all. Just magazines and some paperwork on Solange's pristine desk. Hmmmmm... Her eyes fell onto a file and she flicked it out to see what it was.

It was headed ***Top Secret – The Summer Collection!*** Her eyes widened in amazement. She flicked the pages... lots of drawings of cats wearing... Monsieur le Fluffy's creations!!

She giggled to herself. Clawde and Arfur would be very pleased with her if she brought this home with her! Cunningly she slipped it into her House of Le Claw Pawbag and marched out of the library. She saw her stepmother-in-law's servant in the hall. He was using his bushy tail to sweep the floor.

'Tell OLD Solange that I can't wait... I have too much to do. I'm a busy cat. I will talk with her some other time.' And she stormed off, giggling at the memory of using the corner of Solange's Purrsian rug as a litter tray...''

And I laughed and laughed. Kimmy had been such an inspiration to me and her personality had always made me laugh. Writing the part of Kimmy as Clawdette had been so easy. She was the most wonderful best friend. It was why she had so many fans.

It would all need editing and proofreading but this was going to be a labour of love.)

7th November 2010

(Note from Christine – It was a lovely winter day - crisp and cold outside with bright sunshine – just how I like it to be, and I fed Kimmy, bought the papers and then decided it was too good a day to sit around, so I chose to go for a long walk along the beach to the shops. Usually I would cycle, but today I wanted to linger and enjoy the weather.

Gloriously, the tide was out, so I could amble the whole length of the strand – about two miles of rocky sand – looking out to Belfast Lough and taking in what could be the last beautiful day of the year. I enjoyed the feel of the sunshine and how good it felt to be alive and out on such a day as this.

The shops were busy but it didn't stop me from buying a few things and fighting through the food hall in Marks and Spencer to buy Kimmy's favourite chicken slices and packets of cat food.

I shared a taxi home with a stranger I met at the bus stop. He too had been caught out by the poor Sunday bus timetable and, as we were both going to more or less the same place, we decided to call a taxi and share. At my front door he refused to take any money and that just added to my enjoyment of the day.

As I let myself in, Kimmy came running towards me, indignant for food, and I didn't disappoint. I cut the chicken into small pieces and watched with pleasure as she ate them. But my pleasure turned to worry when I saw that she was automatically pushing the food to one side of her cheeks only and turning her face sideways to try and eat it. It didn't look right and, although I had known for a while now that she sometimes found eating difficult, this looked harder than ever. I made a mental note to tell Naomi when I saw her, for Kimmy's appointment on Thursday, and made a silent prayer that we would get that far. I had already noticed that her tumour was larger and her tongue seemed to loll more out of the side of her mouth. She was no longer able to clean herself and the white area around her bib was very dirty. She also dribbled non-stop. These were not good signs and were signs that Pete had asked me to look out for, but as long as she was eating and didn't appear to be in any pain then we were OK. Now though she looked as if she could be having some pain.

Suddenly the joy of the day seemed to be over and I could see it was clouding over outside, darkening with low clouds forming. A storm was coming.

My early start, long walk and sudden attack of anxiety made me feel tired and I decided to take the newspapers into the bedroom and read them there. This was where I could be sure of Kimmy's company, as she always jumped on the bed to be close to me and pushed her head into my hand to be stroked; she would purr and the two of us would doze happily – but today she wasn't interested and seemed to want to go out. How could she possibly when it was so stormy and cold out there?

Warning her about the storm, I opened the window and climbed back onto the bed. Kimmy would be able to come and go now as she pleased – but I hoped she would join me.

I dozed fitfully and, after a fairly short while, woke to find a dark shadow at the window looming over me. I sighed happily – this would be Kimmy returning from a run in the garden. I had left the window open for her. She would brace herself for the jump and soon she would be on the bed. I would feel the weight of her as she landed... but my eyes adjusted from their sleep and I gave a scream. This wasn't Kimmy at all, but the big bully cat, Guinness, about to jump onto my bed. I jumped up and tried to shake him off the window frame, but he held on tight. I could see Kimmy behind me running under the bed – but unusually she wasn't hissing or yowling – it was as if she had lost the energy to even engage in a play fight. I finally managed to shut the window on Guinness and he flopped down onto the window ledge where he stared in at us menacingly for some time. I could even see the shape of him through the pulled curtain.

I tried to coax Kimmy out from under the bed and, when she did come out, I gave a startled cry to see a great line of blood coming from her mouth. Had she been in a fight with that cat? Had she? And then came the horrible realisation: Kimmy hadn't been fighting – the blood was mixed up with the drool. This was her tumour bleeding, just as I had been told it would – eventually. This was a very bad sign.

All I could think of was Kimmy and what to do next. I grabbed a face cloth from the bathroom and wrung it out under a hot tap and then I chased and caught Kimmy, picked her up and pressed the cloth to her face. She didn't like it one bit and wriggled to get away. I felt terrible doing this to her and watched as she ran under the bed. I knelt beside it and tried to see what she was doing. She was still bleeding.

I rushed to my laptop and emailed Pete Wedderburn and he replied very fast, especially considering it was a Sunday.

Don't worry too much Christine – the blood doesn't mean that it's any more uncomfortable for her, so no need to rush to emergency vet. But sadly, yes, it may mean that it's time to think about final plans tomorrow or the next day.

Nothing easy about this bit – it's the other side of the coin – the payback for all the love and happiness you've shared with her –- unavoidable but no less painful or difficult for being so.... Enjoy her and celebrate her life while she's with you still. Think of all the positives.....

I stared at his email trying to work out how many 'signs' I now had. First there was the increase in size of the tumour, then the extra dribbling, the difficulty she now had eating, the filthiness of her general appearance and the matting on her coat, the lolling tongue and now she was bleeding...

I called the emergency vet and left a message with his service. By now the storm was blowing a gale outside and the rain was lashing against my windows.

He called me within minutes of receiving the message and by then I was crying and had to try and stumble out all that had happened, culminating in the bleeding this afternoon.

The vet was kind and gentle with me and slowly he took in what I was saying.

'Has she eaten?' he asked and I replied that she had eaten well that day but with obvious difficulty.

'I don't think I need come out tonight,' he said, agreeing with Pete. 'If she has eaten today then it's OK, but I do think you should think of bringing her in tomorrow or arranging for a vet to come out, as it does sound as if her cancer is now making her

life very difficult for her. I sobbed my thanks and said I would try to contact Naomi the next day to see what she thought, to decide whether I should bring her in to her open surgery the following evening. The vet said he would email Naomi and tell her of our concerns. We hung up and I felt relief that, whatever else happened, at least I had one last night with her and maybe, just maybe, tomorrow she would, in some way, be better. 'If she eats we're OK,' I told myself firmly, putting food out for her.

But if I had hoped to spend a cosy evening with her lovingly curled up in my lap then I was sorely disappointed. She wouldn't come near me and sat mainly outside the room in the corridor, and if I tried to approach her, she would flinch. I had read somewhere that, if a cat is in pain, they keep their distance, and it looked as if she was in pain.

Mindlessly I watched whatever was on TV, staring at the box but not even knowing or caring what I was watching. I can't tell you now what it was. Kimmy watched me from afar but wouldn't come near.

At about nine p.m, she got restless and hurried over to the front window, desperate to get out, and my heart sank. The wind outside was near hurricane force and the rain was as bad. She couldn't possibly want to go out in that. And then I had a thought – a dreadful one. When cats are in pain or know they are dying they want to run off and hide somewhere. Perhaps to die there? I couldn't let Kimmy out to die in the storm, without me to comfort her. But she was very persistent, pacing and mewing and showing great urgency.

'OK... OK... so you want to go and leave me!' I said impatiently, opening the window and scarcely able to believe what I was doing. I was letting my beloved cat out into a

terrible storm when quite possibly she was in pain. But this could have been her last night and I felt that, whatever else I did, I must let her do whatever she wanted, and if that meant letting her out in a storm (which cats often enjoy), then that is what I should do. And if she wanted to run off somewhere to die then who was I to stop her?

With a heavy heart I watched her run off and I sank into the sofa with a nearly broken heart, trying to make the time pass until she came home – if she came home.

Later I opened the bedroom window and began to get ready for bed, wondering if I should go out with a torch to find her.

But after forever – possibly an hour or more – I heard her thumping in through the window, soaked to the skin. But she had come back – she'd come back to me. There was some great comfort in that, I thought, as I dried her with a towel.

8 November 2010

I really don't feel so well today. My mouth is sore and I can't eat. When I sleep I dream of Bath Cats and Dogs Home… The Pink House in Bath… Mum and I snuggling in bed… hiding in cupboards… tissue paper…crossing the sea on a strange boat and the feel of green grass under my paws. And I dream of flying.

(Note from Christine – This is the hardest bit of the book for me to write by far and I think it may be very hard for you to read, so if you want to, please skip on to the next chapter – Rainbow Bridge. I am sharing it because I owe it to Kimmy and it may help me to make sense of it all. It may also help you

to understand what happens at the 'end' if you don't already know.

I woke early, due to the comings and goings of Kimmy through the window, and she wanted food and wanted to eat, so I staggered from bed and prepared a dish for her, carefully syringing in the pain relief medication. I put the dish down and Kimmy walked away giving me a plaintive look – she couldn't or wouldn't eat it. I tried a second dish – something very different this time and put it down – also noting the uneaten dishes that were there already. I picked them up. But Kimmy wouldn't or couldn't eat the second dish and my heart lurched inside me. I had always said, 'When she doesn't eat, it is time to call the vet.' I put some cat milk down, but she walked away and hid under the bed – withdrawing from me.

It was time and I knew it. All the signs were there – she couldn't eat, her tumour was visibly larger and her mouth more twisted, and to make it worse, she was now bleeding from the tumour. She was withdrawn and almost 'angry' with me, as if in some way blaming me for not being able to help her.

The vet rang soon after nine while I was still in my dressing gown, too muddle-headed to dress. I'd emailed them the night before and they'd heard from the emergency vet. 'Can you bring her in to Ballyclare this morning?' they were asking. I couldn't – I just couldn't. It was not only too soon to give me time to mentally prepare but Ballyclare was the larger vet hospital some six miles away. I'd have to get someone to take me, get dressed fast and catch Kimmy, put her in her hated box and take her on a stressful car journey, perhaps wait in a waiting room full of healthy animals and owners all laughing and happy with joy at their pets. In all the thinking I had done about how 'the end' would happen, this had never been part of the picture. I asked if I could bring Kimmy to Naomi's evening surgery a mile up the road, where she was more used to going. There was a pause and the nurse said she would get back to me. I knew what the difficulty was with this – Naomi's Monday evening surgery was an open one and could get very busy – possibly not the time to give the loving care that this would take. So, I asked about a home visit and Kelly, the vet nurse, said she would speak to Naomi and call me back.

Never had a morning dragged more. It seemed that every time I looked at the clock, no time at all had gone by. I prayed that Kimmy would wander into the living room, ask for food and show me that she was OK for another day. (I judged everything a day at a time.) But Kimmy withdrew more under the bed and flinched when I tried to touch her.

Naomi phoned me late in the morning, her voice full of sorrow for me.

'This has come round fast hasn't it?' she said.

'Are you surprised?' I asked, curious.

'No. It is often this way with this type of tumour.'

Naomi explained her concern about the Monday surgery and said she was worried that she may not be able to find the time for me. She was going to find a nice, kind vet to come out – as she wasn't able to – and if that wasn't possible she suggested bringing Kimmy in ahead of the evening's surgery. She asked if I had managed to get Kimmy to take a tranquiliser in her food and I said that I hadn't, so she said, if a vet did come out, she would ask that they give her a tranquiliser shot first to relax her before she got the main injection. I was grateful for this but was crying so much I couldn't speak.

So once more I waited to find out which would be the best option. I don't think – or didn't think – that it made a good deal of difference being a home visit or a surgery visit, given that the surgery was so close.

Kelly called soon after to say she had found a nice, kind vet called Keith who would come to my flat between three and four p.m. I blurted out that I needed to be sure and that I wanted her examined. I would far rather pay for a home visit and be left with Kimmy if I had not timed this right – rather than have her put to sleep too early.

I spent the rest of the long day on the Internet taking advice, mainly from Pete Wedderburn, who sent me kind and thoughtful messages. He was sure it was 'time.' I also had many, many messages from friends on Facebook who were offering words of comfort. So many of them had been visiting Kimmy's page on a regular basis to see how she was – such is the love that people felt for her.

Mum arrived at lunchtime, bringing a sandwich, but I couldn't eat it. I had been unable to manage breakfast either – my mouth felt dry and I was unable to chew or swallow, but I did pour myself a small glass of wine to try and deaden the horrible feeling I had. It didn't work.

We tried to make mindless conversation while we waited: a long, seemingly eternal wait. But neither us knew what to say so I busied myself by checking email and trying to tidy the flat up a bit for a visitor.

I knew that, on some level, I was still praying that Kimmy would just walk into the room and be OK and I could call the vet and cancel the visit – but it didn't happen. Pete advised me to go in to her and get down on my hands and knees and talk to her – ask her how she was and if she was ready to go. I found this quite outstandingly painful and the reaction I got was Kimmy pulling away and withdrawing further under the bed, turning her back away from me and the finely chopped ham I had taken in with me. Was this her answer?

The clock ticked by slowly and, when we got close to three o'clock, I told Mum that I would get Kimmy out from under the bed and put her in her carrier. She was always so scared of strangers that she would go into deep hiding when she heard Keith arrive, and I couldn't bear having to chase her round to drag her to him. But grabbing her now was not so different. I leaned down beside the bed; she was sitting quite close to the side of it – not far under. She looked listless and her head looked a bit limp. She was either feeling very poorly indeed or she was in pain – and I honestly think she was in pain, as she was purring softly but not looking happy, and I know that cats purr when they are in pain as well as when they are content. I reached under the bed and pulled her hard towards me, cursing myself for my roughness, but she was out and I carried her firmly to her carrier, kissing her head as I did so and speaking soothingly to her.

Once in her carrier – her favourite blanket added – and with it firmly closed, I carried her into the living room to be with Mum and me, while we spoke to her as gently and kindly as we could. I tried to reassure her that she wasn't going anywhere and that someone was coming to make her feel better. And we carried on waiting.

Three o'clock had come and gone and so had three thirty – then it got to four and I was becoming distraught. Why wasn't he here? How much longer could I keep her confined to her carrier?

The phone rang and it was Keith. He was lost. A casual typing error on Kimmy's records meant that someone had transposed a letter in our address. He had gone to a very similar but different address some miles away. I corrected the mistake and accepted his apology. He would be another five or ten minutes – but we all knew it would be longer.

It was darkening dramatically outside and a storm was brewing – it fitted my mood exactly and for some reason I thanked God that it wasn't bright sunshine. I couldn't bear to lose Kimmy on a beautiful day. It was right that it should be dark and stormy. It was fitting.

Keith arrived and I greeted him at the door, clocking that he was wearing his green vet's uniform and that he wasn't carrying a bag or anything. He looked nice and kind and must have seen how tearful I was as he introduced himself and came inside.

He was kind and knelt down by Kimmy as we got her gently from her box. She tried to run off, but I caught her and held her firm. He looked inside her mouth and she seemed to yelp as if in great pain. She had never liked her mouth being examined before but had never made that noise.

Inside her mouth it was distressingly clear what was wrong. The tumour had horribly distended one side of her face so her jaw and teeth no longer met anywhere and the skin tissue looked white and pulpy. Keith explained that she couldn't eat anymore, as she no longer had any sort of 'bite' and, in her attempts to eat, she was pressing on the tumour, making it bleed. 'Left like this, she would starve,' he said grimly but very gently. He went on to say that if he went away without doing anything he would be very unhappy to leave her like this and he was certain I would end up calling again the next day. She had lost at least two of the main criteria that were necessary for keeping a cat alive: she couldn't eat and her quality of life had gone. He also thought she was probably in pain – the third one.

So there was nothing for it but to ask him to go ahead and do what he had to do. This was the part that had haunted me for the past nearly three months and almost took my breath away with shock and horror. It had to be done so could it be quick now please?

There are formalities, which I didn't know about then. Keith asked me to sign a form agreeing that Kimmy should be put to sleep and asking what to do with her remains – I could have them left for burial or she could be cremated. I asked for cremation. And then I had to choose what type of casket I wanted. As I wanted to scatter her ashes (at Mum's) I asked for the cardboard type casket, as I didn't intend keeping the ashes on a mantelpiece or anything. I was told that I would get the ashes back in about two weeks – and that felt about right. Too early would have been too painful and longer would just feel like forever. I hated this part, as Kimmy was still very much alive and I didn't want to discuss this in front of her – but it is a formality which has to be done and I am sure it is a part the vet hated every bit as much as me.

He left the room and went to his car – the wind howling now as the door was opened and closed and I carried on trying to comfort Kimmy in her carrier.

He returned with an injection – the tranquilliser injection to relax her – and asked when she had last eaten. I said not at all that day. It makes a difference, as it can make them vomit. We lifted the lid off the box as Kimmy, stubborn to the last, wouldn't come out. Her last bit of safety was removed and she was exposed to us all. Keith inserted the needle into her scruff and she began to relax almost immediately. I was able to then lift her out of her little sanctuary and hold her in my arms as I sat in an armchair. Relaxed, she snuggled into me and gave me the love that somehow she had been unable to over the past twenty-four hours or so. A warm feeling of love and gratitude swept over me and I thanked God and the vet for allowing me unexpected bit of joy at such a sad time. My tears began to fall as I held her and told her how much I loved her. Kissed her head and promised that she would feel no pain. I noticed that already she seemed cleaner, as if she was halfway to Heaven already – or maybe her adventure in the rain the previous night had cleaned her up a bit. Her whole body felt soft and relaxed and I am sure that – for that short time – she was happy. Mum looked on, her face filled with the sort of sorrow I was feeling. Keith returned with the syringe – a much bigger needle – and I shielded Kimmy's face by pulling her closer to my breast and shoulder and stroking her little head. If Keith was moved by the scene on his return he said nothing but knelt down and pressed the needle into her side, commenting on how well covered she was (although she had lost a good deal of weight). It made me smile just a little, but it seemed to take forever for the injection to go in, although it was probably only seconds. I felt Kimmy give a little gasp – like a cry. And I held her even harder, asking the vet how long before it took effect. 'Oh I am sorry,' he said. 'I should have told you – she's gone already. It just takes a few seconds.' I gave a short wail as I held her close to me and felt her body, limp in my arms, moisture, where her mouth had been, seeping through my shirt. Her eyes were still open and I thought they would close. My beautiful Kimmy had gone.

'Would you like a second alone together?' he asked, holding a stethoscope to her chest.

'Are you sure she's gone?' I asked and he nodded.

I didn't want a 'second' – I couldn't bear to see her dead, limp body and feel the horrible pain of knowing it was all over. I wanted her alive again or to be able to remember her alive – not like this. I think perhaps a day or so later, I wish I had spent a little time talking to her and stroking her, as we don't know when the spirit leaves the body – although I would say hers had gone.

So they don't actually go to sleep as such. Their eyes don't close and the little cry I heard was her heart and organs stopping. It does take just seconds – perhaps four or five, but whether it is totally painless I can't say. It was however a good deal less painful than the death most of us will have and less painful than if the cancer had gone any further.

At that point I just wanted the vet to go. Mum was talking to him while I sat gently crying in the chair where I had held Kimmy. She'd been wrapped in a towel, and her blanket, and put back in the carrier for the vet to take away, but I didn't want to see her go. I just wanted to be alone with my grief and I wanted Mum to go too. The vet had another similar visit to make after this one. I felt for him and had some insight into how hard a vet's job is.

I looked at the clock. It had just gone five, so the vet had been with us for about forty minutes. Mum was very upset – and took a taxi home, as she felt too distressed to drive. I needed to be alone.

I wanted to get online and tell Kimmy's friends and find some comfort. Telling people she was dead was a 'rite of passage' that I had to get out of the way. I emailed Pete first, as he had been so kind throughout, and on this final day, and then I emailed as many people as I could before putting a notice on Facebook. Replies came thick and fast and Jan phoned from Bath in tears and we cried together. Karyn phoned and we cried again. She asked if she could come round and I said 'no' – I needed to be alone. Her cat Flossie also had cancer and I knew that she was thinking of what lay ahead for her, so I was glad I could tell her a bit about it.

Naomi called and said she was glad in a way it hadn't been her, as she would have cried. She said Keith was a more practical person and she offered her condolences. I could barely speak but made sobbing noises and she asked if I had someone with me, but I told her I needed to be alone.

Then I replaced the handset and wondered what to do with myself for the rest of the evening, with a storm howling outside, and I got my reply quickly. My friend Karan Henderson tapped on the window bearing flowers and a card and I gladly let her in, realising that sometimes friends know what we want even when we don't know ourselves. I was so glad to see her and I called Karyn and she came round too. We spent the evening drinking (too much), talking and remembering Kimmy and all the little souls we had lost over the years. In short – we had a wake. The death of a loved pet is very hard to take whatever way you do it, but the way your cat lived its life is far more important – and is what you will remember.

And so, on the 8th November 2010 – the gloomiest month, on the gloomiest hour at around five p.m – my beloved cat, Kimmy, died peacefully in my arms.

Never before did a modest-sized flat feel so big and so empty.)

RAINBOW BRIDGE MISSION FOR KIMMY:

The Kimmy Flight

It is a tradition, on United Cats, for cats who die to be escorted to the Rainbow Bridge by other living cats known as Super Cat Heroes. This was started on United Cats by the amazingly imaginative Elizabeth Ann Scarborough (Ann).

After Kimmy died we had two rainbow escorts for her – one on Facebook and another one on United Cats. I have amalgamated the two here to show you. You have to try to imagine this as a series of blogs with pictures of the cats in their super hero costumes, led by Supurr Cisco, Ann's cat.

<u>Elizabeth Ann Scarborough</u> Cat up and fly on the left side of Kimmy. It will no doubt help her spirit make the adjustment if you keep telling her how fabulous she's going to look with wings and how the rainbow light will be so flattering to her complexion. Betsey, ple… ase take Jamie's paw for the flight or I don't think the little fellow will make it.

V & V would you please take the position immediately to

The cats as superheroes
Heroes costumes designed by Elizabeth Ann Scarborough

Kimmy's rear, behind Mickey and Pancho? Boots and I will fly vanguard.

Everybody ready? Looks like you're all gathered already for the vigil. Up up and AWAAAAAYY!

Sheleg and Jee Jee, at Kimmy's request are helping Superlou and Mr carry a clone of Mugger's magic shield, with a few of Kimmy's outfits and toys on it, in case she CAN take it with her.

Pancho whispers: OMG Kimmy, I can already hear Kittibits and the Late Great Treat, the kitten chorus on harp and student bagpipes starting a melody in your honour with THE STAR OF COUNTY DOWN (never mind the geography, it's the star part that counts, of course). Kimmy, I know this seems like a bummer but honestly, a little white gown and a pair of wings are going to look FABULOUS on mew darling and the rainbow light is very becoming to the complexion. Have mew noticed? Your white tummy is going to reflect it marvellously. And mew can eat ANY time ANYthing mew want. So why am I crying and mopping my eyes with my cape? Because my tail is soaked, that's why. Love mew Kimmy. Mew were the best fake soap opurrah wife a cat of ambiguous sex appeal could have ever had.

Marketa V and V are here and we are flying with Kimmy for the last time.

Sheleg We are here too. Sheleg and Jee Jee. We loved Kimmy dearly and it is very sad for all of us over here.

Teri We are here. Superlou and Superboots and Mr.

PeteW Gladstone's already at the Rainbow Bridge waiting to greet her. Spin and Couscous are both going to go half way with her to make sure she's OK. Gladstone says it's a good place to be – he was released five years ago when he had cancer, so he knows.

Oldwoman SuperSidney is here too to pay tribute to sweet Kimmy.

Connie Goeson She will be missed by many but she will be together with so many of her Rainbow Bridge friends. Her star will shine forever.

Nasshi We are here. Poor Kimmy and her poor Mom. Supertachio, Angus Amazing, Super Schneezy and Romeo the Roarrior poink to join the journey.

Marketa Zvelebil We are flying with her.

<u>Teri Offield</u> Boots has tears in her eyes and sees that Cisco does too. This is a sad day.

Kimmy joins the group a bit angrily. She has a small snack with her, as always. 'I was almost there. I know the way. What kept you?' (SHE IS LOOKING ESPECIALLY ATTRACTIVE AND SHE KNOWS IT).

<u>Elizabeth Ann Scarborough</u> Pancho says, 'Yes Kimmy, but we thought mew would like to be the star this time instead of one of the gang. Mew can still fly missions with us fur other cats, of course, but this is YOUR mission. The Kimmy flight.

<u>Christina Almedida</u> Kimmy is a star here and on the Rainbow Bridge!

<u>Connie Goeson</u> Yes, it is very true that Kimmy is a gorgeous girl. She always looks perfectly groomed and boy is she smart too!

<u>Sidmeow</u> SupuCikoss and Tuki are here. Ciko wipes his tears as he sees Kimmy's spirit. 'Ah you are still an annoying girl!' Tuki says and she runs to hold Kimmy. 'I'll miss you a lot.' Kimmy smiles and wipes the tears on Tuki's face. This escort would be the most memorable one.

<u>Mara Kitty Strydom</u> Silver can't hold her tears but everyone in the kitten-dom is here, even Ash is playing nice. Anything for Kimmy.

<u>Karyn Stapleton</u> Truffles, Fudge, Flossie and Skippy have joined the escort. We are all so sad to hear this news. Fly high Kimmy and enjoy the Bridge. Adieu to a wonderful and unforgettable cat.

<u>The Kimmy Diaries for Fans of Kimmy</u> All corners of the world are here. America, South Africa, England, Denmark, Canada…

<u>Charlotte Hartung Nolsoe</u> Kimmy! You look divine, Bella says. You always had real star quality!

<u>Pamela Cliff</u> All the gang are here. So sad. Xxx

<u>Jan Clare</u> Mickey is high up next to Kimmy with Pancho so we are flying as fast as we can to catch up. Kimmy has made so many of these flights herself over the years with other cats. It is so sad that we finally have to escort her. We shall miss you Kimmy. Our hearts are breaking tonight. Take care. There is so much love for you. We hope you can feel it. We will all meet up again one day. Until then take care. Cassie, Porsche. Jazz and your tomfurriend, Mickey. Xxx

<u>Kitty</u> Patches is here too.

<u>Teri Offield</u> Kimmy you need to go with us and be the STAR that you are! Boots puts her arm around her friend.

<u>Jenny Perrin</u> Ready to go, dear friend. Jules, Cleo, Merly and Arwen fall in behind. She will be the brightest star.

<u>Roni Perotin</u> Tigger, Princess, Zeus and Miracle are all ready to go.

Princess picks up her cell phone but can't hear the meowing of her old furriend Kimmy. Tigger is in dire need of a makeover but 'his woman' is no longer here. Princely Zeus covers his nose with his paw upon hearing the news and Miracle just stares in total disbelief.

<u>Lacey O'Brien</u> Patches pats her eyes once more. She is very sad, but Kimmy will be the most beautiful angel kitty.

<u>Hazel Daska Ibanez</u> Missi is here to escort Kimmy to the Rainbow Bridge.

<u>Pam Edwards</u> Tuffy, Cinny and Gelly here, tears leaking from their eyes. Tuffy is taking it the hardest – his sobs so loud they almost drown out the Late Great Treat.

Kimmy rushes to join her friends but her spirit is no longer visible as she is almost at the Bridge.

<u>Elizabeth Ann Scarborough</u> In the distance, Mrs Kimmy's Mom can be heard quietly sobbing. Pancho poinks back to Kimmy's house and sits on Mrs Kimmy's Mom's chair beside her, with his front paws on her lap and his head available for petting. 'I'm bringing mew these purrs from Kimmy, Mrs Kimmy's Mom. She says thank you so much for… everything. She knows you still love her still and will never furget her and likewise, she's sure. As soon as she has the Rainbow Bridge well under her paw she'll visit sometimes and oh, do hurry with her book please. She wants to show off to the other rainbow cats when she has her next book signing.

Even Pete Wedderburn joined in with the spirit of it all and, in those dark days that followed Kimmy's death, it was an enormous comfort, as were the dozens of emails that poured in from Kimmy's many fans and friends.

Reading it back now still makes my eyes moist. Thank you so much to all who took part.

22nd November 2010

The surgery called to tell me that Kimmy's ashes were ready for collection and I braced myself for the sadness of this moment. Ginger, my pet psychic, had emailed me that morning to say that she had 'seen' Kimmy surrounded by lots of food and then jumping in the bedroom window on to something like a wicker chair before taking up position on my bed.

"Christine, I saw 1,000 Kimmys and 1000 bowls of food. She was trying to tell me she is happy eating all of the kibble she can! I did "see" a kitchen-like chair in your bedroom & she jumped in the window, walked by the chair & gets up and down on your bed. Like over and over so you know she's there. She sees you cry. Our pets want us to be happy. When you feel ready, keep your heart open to love another kitty. Kimmy won't be mad. I will put you on my healing list this week to try to lighten your heart. Peace & blessings Ginger"

This was another huge comfort and I found myself believing what Ginger said. How would she know that this was how Kimmy always came in and out of my apartment – she couldn't know it was ground floor and had no cat flap. Or that the wicker chair is a linen chest that she used to jump down onto from the open window before jumping onto my bed. I had been sleeping with the window open at night for as long as I could – in the hope that her spirit would come in – and this seemed to confirm it. I liked the bit about the food and felt sure that, if Kimmy was anywhere like Rainbow Bridge, she would be surrounded by food!

I was going to cycle to the vet to pick up Kimmy's ashes, but I remembered something that Mara Strydom had said ages before on Facebook when she heard I liked to ride my bike. 'I could just see you on your bike with Kimmy at the front in a basket,' she had said. The thought of this image had made us laugh at the time and had made me smile over the years, but now the thought of it actually coming true – me cycling with her ashes in the pannier – was just too distressing, so I took a cab. When I got there, the receptionist was cradling Kimmy –

now in a cylindrical box – and I felt fresh tears again when I realised how everyone had loved her. It surely couldn't be her in this cardboard box, could it? I paid the bill for the home visit and the cremation and hoped I would hold back the tears until I had brought Kimmy home for the last time. I put her ashes first on the mantelpiece near the fire, where she had loved toasting her tummy so much, and later, by my bed, where they felt more appropriate.

A few months later, in the spring, Karyn and Fred's cat, Flossie, died – nearly a year after her cancer diagnosis. And on a beautiful sunny morning I felt able to scatter Kimmy's ashes in her favourite strawberry bush, now planted with forget-me-nots, in Mum's garden where she'd been so happy.

"The soul takes flight to the world that is invisible but there arriving she is sure of bliss and forever dwells in paradise."
Plato

I once asked my friend Karan Henderson if she'd think of getting a pet and she said she wouldn't because she couldn't bear to go through what I was going through, losing Kimmy.

I told her 'This is nothing. Compared to all the love and fun we get from them over the years, a few weeks or even months of intense pain at their loss is totally worth it.'

And I meant it.

Epilogue

I had intended to wait until after Christmas before even thinking of getting another cat. Kimmy wasn't the sort of cat I could just go out and 'replace' and I needed proper time to grieve for her. But we had a very cold spell of snow and frost and the Mid Antrim Animal Sanctuary, close to my home, had extremely basic accommodation at the time (prior to recent rebuilding). When I thought of the animals, living in little more than sheds, in such freezing weather, and I looked at my warm but very empty flat, I found myself taking a taxi out there, less than three weeks after Kimmy died. I can honestly say that Ollie chose me. I looked down at the concrete floor and found a ginger face staring up at me whilst touching my foot with his paw. Ollie had previously been brought in when his student owners had moved and been unable to take him. He was just a year old. I thought it would take a while for him to settle with me and for me to grow to love him, but that very night – when he scrambled onto my bed and pushed his small body close to my legs – I felt that overwhelming comfort you get from living with a little creature. We moved soon after that to a new house just across the road – Kimmy would have loved it, with its big, private garden with mature trees all around. It felt like we had her with us because it felt like she was already there.

A year later he was joined by Minnie – a cat I adopted after her family moved away and left her to fend for herself – and two years after that, a ginger kitten was brought to my Mother's house for re-homing and guess where he (Ted) finished up?

I caught Guinness and took him to the vet for neutering. I had no idea how this would turn out, but let's just say the whole neighbourhood offered to chip in for the operation! He disappeared not long after and, of course, I feared the worst. In desperation, I put posters up around the area and was surprised to get a call from a lovely lady called Jane Dykes to tell me that she had Guinness (only she called him Kurt). He slept in her greenhouse, but she was scared to bring him in, in case he attacked her three female cats. 'I'd have him neutered,' she said, 'but I'd never be able to catch such a large cat.' I was delighted to tell her that I had had him neutered, and so Kurt got invited inside. He is no longer a pest, fighting with the neighbourhood cats and breaking cat flaps. He's a well-loved lap-cat who is eternally grateful for a loving home – mainly thanks to a wonderfully kind and caring new owner.

Karan Henderson adopted a greyhound from the local pound and is now a devoted owner.

So life goes on and I have three cats instead of one, but not a day goes past that I don't think about and miss my beautiful Kimmy.

About Bath Cats and Dogs Home

"We service an area of over 650 square miles (the size of London) throughout Bath, Somerset and Wiltshire. We accept dogs; cats and small animals in need – lost, abused, sick, injured and unwanted animals are brought in to us by the public, dog wardens and RSPCA inspectors.

We pride ourselves on our non-destruction policy and aim to find every animal a new loving home, no matter how long this may take.

Formed in 1937 from an amalgamation of local rescue groups, we moved to Claverton Down in 1939 and the space has allowed us to expand to house over 100 dogs, 100 cats, 70 chickens and 30 or so rabbits and small animals at any one time.

This makes us one of the busiest RSPCA Branches in the country, re-homing over 1,300 dogs, cats and small animals each year. Like all Branches, we are an independent charity that receives little financial support from the National RSPCA and therefore rely heavily on charitable giving to fund our annual running costs of £1.4 million.

As well as rescuing and re-homing animals in need we play an active role in the local community; attending shows and events throughout the year, giving educational talks in schools and at the Home on the importance of responsible pet ownership and offer volunteering opportunities and work experience to young people and those seeking employment. We also employ over 50 paid members of staff from the local area."

Further Reading

*The Animal Communicator's Guide Through
Life Loss and Love by Pea Horsley, Hayhouse*
ISBN 978-1-78180-334-9

The Kimmy Diaries by Kimmy
ISBN 978-0-7552-0436-6

Kimmy's Irish Diaries
ISBN 978-0-7552-0611-7

Clawless
ISBN 978-0-7552-0657-5

In Memory of Kimmy

- Panga Find
- Press Release
- Society germs —
- Press Articles + — Val
- Polical Build up — This

- 7 Order Nums
-

A T R .   1:11

I 88 R

all apple R

- Pinboard
- Life Magazine
- web sites
chronos / choderp / Pred green

Lightning Source UK Ltd.
Milton Keynes UK
UKOW04f0154111014

239920UK00013BA/149/P

9 780755 207473